ALBEMARLE & CHARLOTTESVILLE

An Illustrated History of the First 150 Years

by Rick Britton

A publication of the Albemarle Charlottesville Historical Society

Historical Publishing Network
A division of Lammert Inc.
San Antonio, Texas

30305 749
S

This book is dedicated to my beautiful wife, Victoria, without whose love and support none of this would have been possible.

ACKNOWLEDGMENTS

The author would like to thank the great staff at the Albemarle Charlottesville Historical Society for their patience and support. Director Douglas Day IV and Assistant Director Sarah Hamfeldt were always willing to help, and careful not to remind me too often of the deadlines. Librarian Margaret M. O'Bryant was invaluable in locating the accompanying images. Summer Intern Gene Lepley was especially helpful in the scanning process. Unless otherwise noted all of the images are from the collection of the Albemarle Charlottesville Historical Society. The beautiful pen and ink sketches on pages 13, 15, 21, 24, 26, 37, and 48 (by H. Heywood and A. Robinson) first appeared in Mary Rawlings's *Ante-bellum Albemarle*.

Special thanks are due the folks at Monticello for their graciousness in granting photographic rights, Special Collections at the University of Virginia for the image of Isaac Jefferson, the Chamber of Commerce for the great Jack Jouett woodcut, Bob Belton for his assistance with the first few chapters, and Bruce Young of Lexington for his great Monticello interiors. While dozens of friends made suggestions concerning the contents, any errors in the text are solely the responsibility of the author.

Cover Photo by Rick Britton.

Photo of the author by Victoria Britton

Monticello Interiors by Master Photographer Bruce Young of Lexington, Virginia.

First Edition

ISBN: 978-1-893619-55-5
Library of Congress Card Catalog Number: 2006927586

Albemarle & Charlottesville: An Illustrated History of the First 150 Years

author:	Rick Britton
cover photographer:	Rick Britton
contributing writers for "Sharing the Heritage":	Joe Goodpasture
	Judi Free

Historical Publishing Network

president:	Ron Lammert
project manager:	Pat Steele
administration:	Angela Lake
	Donna M. Mata
book sales:	Dee Steidle
graphic production:	Colin Hart
	Charles A. Newton, III
	Craig Mitchell
	Michael Reaves
	Evelyn Hart

CONTENTS

4   INTRODUCTION

5   CHAPTER I   Albemarle: the Land & its First People

11   CHAPTER II   Albemarle County: Its Settlement & Formation

18   CHAPTER III   Albemarle in the American Revolution

25   CHAPTER IV   Jefferson, Albemarle's Favorite Native Son

31   CHAPTER V   Years of Prosperity: Albemarle from the 1780s
                         to the 1820s

38   CHAPTER VI   The University of Virginia: The "Hobby"
                         of Jefferson's Old Age

45   CHAPTER VII   Antebellum Albemarle: Slavery and
                         the Coming Fury

52   CHAPTER VIII   Albemarle in the Civil War

61   CHAPTER IX   Albemarle in the Late 1800s: A New Beginning

69   BIBLIOGRAPHY

70   SHARING THE HERITAGE

120   INDEX OF SPONSORS

INTRODUCTION

Much like its clay soil, Albemarle's history is thick with fascinating individuals. Many, naturally, were people who simply passed through these parts, or those who stayed a while, Albemarle's adopted sons and daughters. A good number of these extraordinary folks, however, were native-born. County residents helped map, tame, and govern the Old Dominion. They opened up, explored, and conquered the frontier. They educated America's youth, and they fought and died in Virginia's great struggles.

Following the region's most cataclysmic contest an entire race of newly-freed people put their backs to the daunting effort of starting from scratch. Several local African Americans strode from Albemarle onto much grander stages. In this, of course, they were not alone. Oftentimes, the people of Charlottesville and Albemarle had left their marks on the nation and the globe.

In Albemarle the bar was set very high from the very beginning of European settlement. In 1743, one of the region's first families produced a son—the incomparable Thomas Jefferson—whose crystalline writings sparked a revolution, and over the years brought hope to uncounted millions. Following his two-term presidency, Jefferson retired here to his beloved Monticello and spent much of his later years in the founding of the University of Virginia, one mile to Charlottesville's west.

Perhaps it was Albemarle's stint as part of the Virginia frontier that gave so many of its residents a westward-looking point of view. The discoverer of the Cumberland Gap into Kentucky, Dr. Thomas Walker, lived in the county for a number of years. George Rogers Clark—the "Conqueror of the Northwest"—was born in Albemarle County in 1752. Half a century later Clark's younger brother William explored Louisiana with Meriwether Lewis (who also was a native of Albemarle, born in 1774).

During the American Revolution—at the time when the Virginia General Assembly was on the run from the British army—the little town of Charlottesville, not yet twenty years old, served briefly as the capital of Virginia. Chasing after the legislature and Governor Jefferson, British Lieut. Col. Banastre Tarleton stormed into Charlottesville to find that most had departed, in haste, for Staunton. He did manage to capture, however, a frontiersman who was here representing the county of Kentucky—Daniel Boone.

James Monroe practiced law out of an office in Charlottesville in the late 1780s. Later in his career he helped negotiate the Louisiana Purchase, and as our nation's fifth president warned European nations against interference in the Americas. Monroe owned Highland, in Albemarle County, for over thirty years. Edward Coles—a powerful anti-slavery two-term governor of Illinois—was born in Albemarle in 1786. The Marquis de Lafayette visited in 1824, as part of his Grand Triumphal Tour, and was wined and dined by both Jefferson and Albemarle County. The University of Virginia opened the following year. One of the first students was a thin 17-year-old from Boston named Edgar Allan Poe. A generation later one U.Va. professor, William Holmes McGuffey, compiled a series of *Eclectic Readers* which eventually sold over 120 million copies.

Antebellum Albemarle wrestled with the insidious institution of slavery. When the argument over slavery brought war, Albemarle's sons bled in every major battle fought by Robert E. Lee's Army of Northern Virginia. Hundreds, unfortunately, filled the ranks commanded by Gen. George E. Pickett. One Albemarle native—George Wythe Randolph, Jefferson's youngest grandchild—served briefly as Confederate States' secretary of war.

Attempting to ameliorate the war's pain, Charlottesville and the University treated over 20,000 wounded. In February of 1864 Union Gen. George Armstrong Custer led a raid into Albemarle but was driven back in the county's only real clash of arms. One year later Charlottesville was captured by a cavalry force under Custer and Gen. Philip Sheridan.

The end of the Civil War meant emancipation and reconstruction. For fully half of Albemarle's citizenry Mr. Jefferson's Declaration was finally beginning to come true. Black Baptist churches sprang up. A prominent local black leader, Fairfax Taylor, spoke frequently at political gatherings, demanding equal treatment. James Taylor, his son, was elected in 1867 to the state's constitutional convention.

The late 1800s brought modernization—industry, telephones, and more railroads to connect the Piedmont to the rest of the world. Charlottesville became an independent city in 1888. In the century's final, spasmodic years Mr. Jefferson's gorgeous Rotunda was gutted by fire and one of Albemarle's own was dubbed "the nation's most beautiful blonde."

Thus ended the nineteenth century in central Virginia. But what a time it had been, and what amazing people had walked our streets. Their stories—as well as the tales of the land itself—make up the first 150 years of Albemarle County history.

CHAPTER I

ALBEMARLE: THE LAND & ITS FIRST PEOPLE

*Lying under the evening shadows of the beautiful Blue Ridge, the Piedmont country was abundant in game,
minerals, and a clay-rich soil well-suited to farming. Its first inhabitants were a fascinating people
whose remains attracted the attention of a future president.*

*The Ragged Mountains of
southern Albemarle.*

Located in the central Virginia Piedmont, the land that became Albemarle County was one of promise and plenty. It was a virgin wilderness with many attractions. "The low grounds upon the rivers and creeks are exceedingly rich, being loam intermingled with sand," wrote Andrew Burnaby of a visit to the area in 1759, "and the higher you go up into the country, towards the mountains, the value of the land increases: for it grows more strong, and consists of a deeper clay."

Burnaby noted that Indian corn and tobacco were "the original produce of the country." To the list of the area's native vegetation he added "the pigeon-berry, and rattlesnake root so esteemed…grapes, strawberries, hickory nuts, mulberries, chestnuts, and several other fruits [which] grow wild and spontaneously."

"Besides trees and flowers of an ordinary nature," he continued, "the woods produce myrtles, cedars... firs of different sorts, and no less than seven or eight kinds of oak; they are likewise adorned and beautified with red-flowering maples, sassafras-trees, dogwoods…and innumerable other sorts, so that one may reasonably assert that no country ever appeared with greater elegance or beauty."

Indeed, today's Albemarle still bears innumerable traces of its earlier majesty. Running from the crests of the hazy Blue Ridge Mountains, Albemarle's northwestern boundary, the heavily-forested hills roll southeastward for twenty miles to a parallel, sister range—the Southwest Mountains. Beyond—in the easternmost portion once called the Flatwoods—the clay-soil contours flatten as Albemarle, following the paths of its gurgling streams, stretches out toward the mighty James River and the Virginia Tidewater.

"Besides the James," wrote the Rev. Edgar Woods in 1901 (in Albemarle County's first real history), "the county is cut throughout its entire breadth by two streams, and is washed at its southwest

❖

A western Albemarle stream.

the Hardware pursues a southeast course, and—like the Rivanna to its north—empties into the James. This last-named river forms the southernmost boundary of present-day Albemarle County.

"The character of the soil is various," penned Woods. "The degrees of its fertility are distinguished by different colors, the richest exhibiting a deep red, and the less fertile a gray. The former prevails at the base of the mountains, and along the banks of the streams. Some parts of the county, especially in the mountainous localities, are stony; the more level lands are free from this encumbrance. The prevalent rocks are quartz and what is colloquially known as mountain granite…. The soil and climate of Albemarle are well adapted to all the staple productions of the temperate zone, and are exceedingly favorable to the cultivation of fruit."

Game of every kind was plentiful. Deer, of course, roamed Albemarle in large numbers but so did elk, bears, and even bison. According to Woods, a buffalo trail "is said to have run up the Rockfish River" to Buffalo Gap in the Blue Ridge Mountains. Flocks of turkeys seemingly were everywhere, and every fall and spring flights of wild ducks and geese alit on Albemarle's waters within easy buckshot range. "Tradition," wrote Woods, "refers to more than one pigeon roost, where great limbs of trees were broken down by the countless numbers of that bird. Before the construction of dams, fish of the best kinds, shad and herring, ascended the watercourses."

Those watercourses had been valuable transportation routes for Albemarle's first inhabitants—the Monacan Indians. Thomas Jefferson—writing in 1780 regarding Virginia's "upwards of forty different tribes of Indians"—noted that "the Powhatans, the Mannahoacs, and the Monacans, were the most powerful." He ascribed to the Monacan Nation dominion over the area between the "upper parts of the James River" and the Blue Ridge Mountains (or the "Quiranck" as the Indians called them).

The region controlled by the Monacans, therefore, was vast and fertile. It included the valleys of the James and Rivanna Rivers, and the fabulous country drained by their tributaries both north and south. The Indians of Virginia—especially the Tidewater-based Powhatans who warred against the Monacans—regarded it as a separate and distinct land. Sir Henry Payton,

corner by a third, all of considerable size." The northernmost of these is the Rivanna River (named after Queen Anne, the second daughter of James II and Anne Hyde). The Rivanna gathers its waters from several tributaries, as well as from a robust north fork, then splashes through the Southwest Mountains at Pantops before rushing eighteen miles to its confluence with the James at Point of Fork.

In south central Albemarle the hillocks run off into the Hardware River. This stream has two forks, which join just upwater from its passage through the Southwest Mountains. From there

for example, was inexplicably abandoned sometime in the 1670s.

Unfortunately, the Monacan people left few traces. Their existence is described by but a few first-hand accounts. Only two of their original villages, both on the banks of the James River, were visited by white men. Of Monasukapanough we have no written record. Perhaps the best description of the Monacans came from the hand of John Fontaine, a Huguenot who in 1716 toured a Saponi village established outside of Fort Christianna, in Brunswick County (south of Richmond, near present-day Lawrenceville). It is possible that these people were the direct, lineal descendants—but a few generations removed—of the inhabitants of Monasukapanough, on the Rivanna. What little else we know of the Monacans is based on the assumption that their way of life resembled that of the Powhatans.

The Monacan civilization was a simple one. The men made war, fished, and stalked game through the open woods. Because they maintained no herds or flocks, their hunters ranged over a wide area in search of meat. Deer was their favorite. Bears were also killed for meat after they

Left: A portion of the 1612 John Smith map of Virginia showing the James and Rivanna Rivers, and the location of Monasukapanough.

Below: A typical Native American village enclosed with a palisade.
IMAGE COURTSEY OF THE AUTHOR

writing in 1610, referred to the area as "the Land called the Monscane."

"The Monscane" embraced at least five large Indian towns including Monasukapanough in present-day Albemarle County. This "extensive village"—as archeologist David Bushnell Jr. called it, writing in the 1920s—occupied both sides of the Rivanna River at a beautiful and easily fordable spot two miles above its principal fork. Monasukapanough's inhabitants—numbering possibly as many as 1,200—were members of the Saponi tribe, a "contributor-tribe" of the Monacan Nation.

Exactly when the Monacan people—including the Saponi—first moved to the Virginia Piedmont will, most likely, forever remain a mystery. There is no doubt, however, that they spoke a Siouan language. "The earlier habitat of the Siouan tribes…is believed to have been in the valley of the Ohio," wrote Bushnell, "from which region they crossed the mountains to the eastward…." Perhaps these early Sioux were driven over the Alleghenies by enemies to their north. Perhaps they made the trek in search of better game. In the Piedmont they built villages, multiplied, and remained—until two generations prior to the arrival of the first European settlers in the late 1720s. Monasukapanough,

The towne of Pomeiock and true forme of their howses covered and enclosed some with matts, and some with barcks of trees, All compassid abowt with smale coles stock thick together in stedd of a wall.

had fattened up for their winter sleep. When the nearby wildlife was depleted, the Monacan huntsmen often followed the bison over the Quiranck and into the great valley beyond. The Monacans were also adept fishermen—as were the other Eastern Woodland tribes—and frequently built river weirs, or dams, in order to gather fish in submerged woven baskets.

Monacan women worked as gardeners. Of the vegetables they cultivated, Thomas Jefferson named at least four in his *Notes on the State of Virginia*: pumpkins, squash, corn, and "long" (or sweet) potatoes. Corn was highly prized by the Monacans. One of their favorite trading items, in fact, was a clay pot filled with the golden kernels. Corn and beans they planted together. As the corn stalks sprouted up they provided the runners for the bean vines to climb.

Interestingly, it appears that some Monacan villages resembled the palisaded forts erected by the light-skinned colonists. "[T]he houses join all the one to the other, and altogether make a circle," Fontaine wrote of the Saponi/Monacan town he visited. "[The village's outer] walls are large pieces

run through their ears, their faces painted with blue and vermilion, their hair cut in many forms, some on one side of the head, and some on both, and others on the upper part of the head making it stand like a cock's-comb...." These proud warriors—wrapped in blue and red blankets—strutted about in their "abominable dress," looking for all the world, wrote Fontaine, "like so many furies." The Monacan women had long, straight black hair reaching down to their waists. They used nothing to cover their upper bodies but each of them wore,

Top: Typical Monacan pottery shards.

Middle: Monacan weapons and tools.

Bottom: Indian shards found near Monasukapanough.

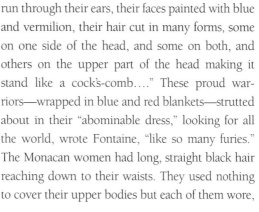

of timber which are squared, and being sharpened at the lower end, are put down two feet in the ground, and stand about seven feet [high]. These posts are laid as close together as possible...."

To protect themselves from the weather "they make a roof with rafters," wrote Fontaine, "and cover the house with oak or hickory bark, which they strip off in great flakes, and lay it so closely that no rain can come in." Other Saponi shelters were described as being circular, made up of a framework of flexible saplings—with both ends firmly secured in the ground—the whole covered with bark or grass mats. Across the entranceway would be hung a deerskin. These abodes must certainly have been dark and smoky affairs—one portal providing the only light while one hole in the roof, the only escape for the smoke rising from the inevitable fire which was, according to Fontaine, "always in the middle of the house."

Although these people had constructed shelters and inhabited a common village their lives were otherwise fairly spare. "[T]he chief of their household goods is a pot and some wooden dishes and trays, which they make themselves," wrote the Huguenot tourist. "[T]hey seldom have any thing to sit upon, but squat upon the ground.... These people have no sort of tame creatures, but live entirely upon their hunting and the corn which their wives cultivate. They live as lazily and miserably as any people in the world."

Fortunately Fontaine also described the appearance of the Monacan people at Fort Christianna. For their war dress, the young men of the tribe decorated themselves "with feathers in their hair and

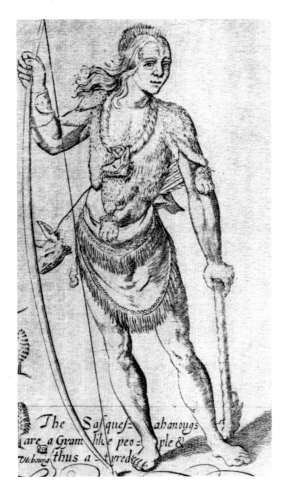

wrote Fontaine, "a blanket tied round the waist, and hanging down about the legs like a petticoat." These women were wild looking and very shy around Europeans.

Like John Fontaine, Jefferson was fascinated by Native Americans, particularly the earlier inhabitants of his native region. Around 1780 he made a personal investigation of the great burial mound that sat near Monasukapanough. The mound "was situated on the low grounds of the Rivanna," penned Jefferson. "It was of spheroidical form, of about 40 feet diameter at the base, and had been of about twelve feet altitude, though now reduced by the plough to seven and a half, having been under cultivation about a dozen years."

Jefferson's systematic dig—which won for him the title "father of modern archeology"—revealed about one thousand skeletons arranged in rough layers with no apparent plan. The bones did not seem to show wounds acquired in battle, and he did not believe that the barrow was simply Monasukapanough's "common sepulchre." Since the prominence contained so many bodies, was it—for a time—the main burial mound for a portion of the Monacan nation? There is evidence that

it was revered, and long remembered, by the Native Americans. Writing in 1780 Jefferson recalled "a party [of Indians] passing, about thirty years ago, through the part of the country where this barrow is, went through the woods directly to it, without any instructions or enquiry, and having stayed about it some time, with expressions which were construed to be those of sorrow, they returned to the high road…and pursued their journey."

Why was Monasukapanough abandoned? We may never know. Possibly the Saponi/Monacans were driven from their lands—toward the southwest, along the North Carolina border—by other Native Americans. Fontaine wrote that "the destructive forays by bands from the Five Nations of New York had kept the Virginia Indians in an uproar for more than a century." Perhaps they retreated to avoid armed conflict with the Europeans.

The Monacan culture left next to nothing in its wake. Their dwellings required but a few indentations in the ground, their clothing and wooden implements have returned to dust. What is left to us is a dim understanding of a once-proud people who ruled the territory overseen by the Mountains Quiranck when it was still very close to its natural state. Long before the Piedmont's stump-studded fields rang with the sounds of the white man's ax, Albemarle was the domain of the Monacan.

CHAPTER II

ALBEMARLE COUNTY: ITS SETTLEMENT & FORMATION

Established in 1744, the county went through several transformations. In these early years its population grew rapidly and tobacco quickly became king. On a hill above the Rivanna, Charlottesville was laid out in 1762.

Batteaux on the James River.

IMAGE COURTESY OF THE AUTHOR

From the beginning, Virginia's colonists were westward-looking people. The first European settlements in the Old Dominion, of course, were nestled alongside the mouths of the Tidewater estuaries. The falls and rapids of the upper rivers—not to mention the mighty Powhatan—were the first great barriers to colonizing the interior. With time the frontier was advanced west, as the Native Americans were squelched and as planting and grazing fields were hacked from the riverside forests. Nonetheless, for over 100 years after the establishment of Jamestown the central Piedmont of Virginia was still virtually a wilderness.

In 1716 Gov. Alexander Spotswood—along with his sixty-some Knights of the Golden Horseshoe—ascended the Rapidan River, traversed the Blue Ridge, and explored the Valley of Virginia. Accounts of the expedition, especially of the fertile lands encountered beyond the fall line, spread far and wide. Within the next twenty years, "a tide of population" swept over Albemarle—as well as the rest of the Piedmont—much of it pushing up the waterways from the east while another, smaller wave lapped over the Blue Ridge after flowing "up" the Shenandoah Valley from the western reaches of Pennsylvania.

"Besides the restless spirit animating the first settlers," wrote the Rev. Edgar Woods, "the occupation of the country was hastened by the rage for speculation. The laws of the colony allotted fifty acres for every person transported into its territory; and men of wealth in addition to availing themselves of this provision, largely invested their means in the purchase of land." Tidewater gentry were Albemarle's first landowners. "The Piedmont frontier," noted historian Emily J. Salmon, "was developed less by poor farmers in search of opportunity than by the colony's leading families, such as the Randolphs, Carters, Pages, and Nicholases, who acquired the best acreage along the rivers."

"As settlement edged toward the Blue Ridge Mountains," wrote Salmon, "the formation of new counties beyond the fall line extended Tidewater institutions into the west." Goochland County—stretching from just west of Richmond to the Blue Ridge—was formed from Henrico in 1728. Hanover, just to the north, had been established eight years earlier. The first settlements within the present bounds of Albemarle, therefore, were established while the land still rested within these two jurisdictions.

Albemarle's first land patents were taken out on June 16, 1727. On that date George Hoomes of Caroline County was granted 3,100 acres "on the far side of the mountains called Chestnut" (i.e., the

Southwest Mountains), while Nicholas Meriwether was granted a massive tract of 13,762 acres. Nearly two years later Dr. George Nicholas patented 2,600 acres on the left bank of the James. The year 1730 saw grants taken out in Albemarle by Allen Howard, Thomas Carr, Charles Hudson, Francis Eppes, and Secretary John Carter totaling a whopping 20,950 acres. Of these 9,350 "on the Great Mountain on Hardware in the fork of the James" (i.e., today's Green Mountains), went to Carter. That same year Nicholas Meriwether was granted an additional 4,190 acres, adjoining his previous patent, bringing his Albemarle holdings to a total acreage of 17,952.

Over the next four years, large patents were obtained by, according to Woods: Charles Lewis, "on both sides of the Rivanna"; Charles Hudson, "on the west side of Carter's Mountain"; Major Thomas Carr, "on the back side of the Chestnut Mountains"; Thomas Goolsby, "on the north side of the Fluvanna" (i.e., the James west of its confluence with the Rivanna); Edward Scott, John Key, Dr. Arthur Hopkins, Charles Lynch, Henry Wood, "the first clerk of Goochland," Edwin Hickman, Joseph Smith, Thomas Graves, Joel Terrell, David Lewis, and Jonathan Clark, grandfather of George Rogers Clark.

"From this time," penned Woods, "the county was settled in greater rapidity.... Few of those [early grantees] occupied their lands, at least in the first instance. They made the clearings and entered upon the cultivation which the law required in order to perfect their titles, but it was done either by tenants, or by their own servants [i.e., slaves], whom they established in 'quarters.' Now, however, a new order of things began." From this time forward Albemarle grants were more frequently obtained by persons who intended to live and farm in the bountiful land between the James and the Blue Ridge. One of these was Peter Jefferson. His son Thomas later referred to him as "the third or fourth settler, about the year 1737, of the part of the county in which I live." Legend has it that the elder Jefferson, after receiving his first land grant, purchased the tract upon which he built Shadwell, the family estate, for the sum total of a bowl of Arrack punch.

The act establishing Albemarle County was passed in September of 1744. It cited "divers inconveniences attending the upper inhabitants of Goochland by reason of their great distance from the

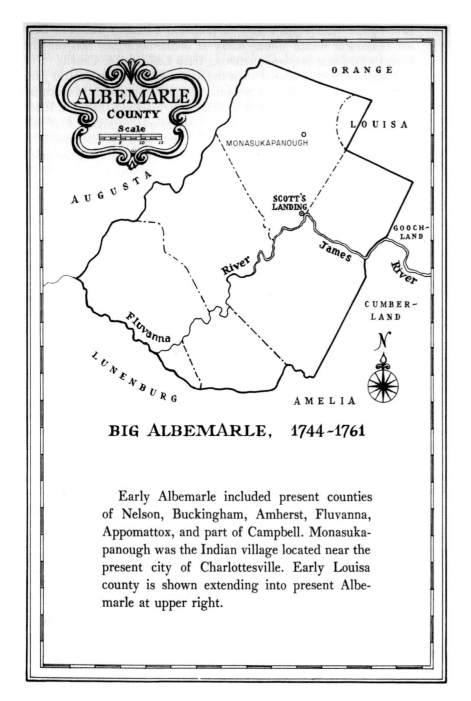

BIG ALBEMARLE, 1744~1761

Early Albemarle included present counties of Nelson, Buckingham, Amherst, Fluvanna, Appomattox, and part of Campbell. Monasuka-panough was the Indian village located near the present city of Charlottesville. Early Louisa county is shown extending into present Albemarle at upper right.

Above, left: "Big Albemarle" illustrated by John Middleton Freeman.

Above, right: William Anne Keppel, Earl of Albemarle.

courthouse." (The newly-created county was named for William Anne Keppel—the second Earl of "Albemarle," an Anglicization of "Aumale," a county in northwestern Normandy—an accomplished man who, though the governor of Virginia from 1737 to 1754, visited neither his namesake county nor his colonial territory.) Taking effect the first day of 1745, this act created what has since been called "Big Albemarle," a vast region embracing present-day Fluvanna, Buckingham, Nelson, and Amherst counties, as well as portions of Appomattox and Campbell. The first version of Albemarle, therefore, included much of the James River valley upstream from the fall line.

Near today's Scottsville—at Totier, a plantation owned by Mrs. Edward Scott—Albemarle County was formally organized in February of 1745. Among those present were Peter Jefferson, Joseph Thompson who was sworn in as sheriff, Edmund Gray who was made King's attorney, and Joshua Fry who became the official surveyor. As well as appointing the county's militia officers, Albemarle's founders authorized Samuel Scott to construct, at his own expense, a courthouse, a prison, and stocks "as good as those of Goochland." This first seat of Albemarle County government was established on the plantation of Daniel Scott, Samuel's brother, about a mile west of today's Scottsville.

Setting up a county can certainly work up a man's thirst. By 1748—within three years of Albemarle's placement on the map—licenses had been issued for over ten ordinaries. Taverns, inns and ordinaries (the names were somewhat interchangeable) were the intermittent way stations providing beverages, food, and rest between the long stretches of infamously bad Virginia road. Of these first businesses, Hugh McGarrough opened one, according to Woods, "not far from Afton," while Daniel Scott and John Lewis each operated taverns, serving up spirits, "at the courthouse." Not to be outdone, William Battersby set one up "opposite the courthouse."

Thomas Jefferson later estimated that the county's population, at its inception, was about 4,250. Within but fifteen years, however, the settlers had so increased in number that they again petitioned for courthouses at more accessible places. Responding to these needs, in March of 1761 the House of Burgesses carved out from Albemarle the new counties of Buckingham and Amherst (which, at the time incorporated Nelson County). Additionally, a portion of western Louisa was, by this same measure, attached to northeastern Albemarle County. (Certain James River islands were added to Albemarle in 1769, while the southeastern portion of the county was lopped off to create Fluvanna County in 1777.) Today's Albemarle County, therefore—comprising 740 square miles—has been in existence since the second year of the American Revolution.)

As the settlers moved into the Piedmont, the Tidewater tobacco economy quickly took root. "Throughout the colonial period," wrote Salmon, "the Virginia Company of London, the Crown, and several royal governors tried to diversify Virginia's economy, but tobacco dominated...." Planters would later complain of the weed ruin-

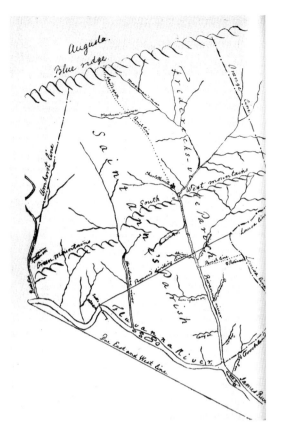

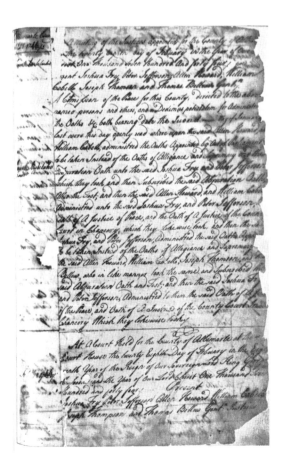

ing their land, but in early Albemarle land was plentiful. The upland tobacco grew best in the nutrient-laden loam of bottomlands and Albemarle possessed many rich river valleys.

[T]obacco requires a heavy and fertile soil," wrote Jacques Pierre Brissot, who visited Virginia in 1788, "and also continual attention in transplanting, weeding, and protecting it from insects that attack it...." Cultivation, although labor

❖

Left: Thomas Jefferson's map of the "Proposed Separation of Fluvanna," 1777.

Bottom, left: A page from the Order Book of the Albemarle County Court, 1744/45-1748.

Bottom, right: Believed by some to be the home of Mrs. Edward Scott where the County of Albemarle was organized.

intensive, required but few implements: only an axe, a plow, and a hoe. An area growing hardwoods—thus demonstrating fertility—was first cleared. Any remaining undergrowth was then burnt away. Next, the earth was plowed and small hills for the tobacco plants were hoed up. In Albemarle "tobo" grew fast, and once grown was quickly dried in the sun, and packed into large casks called hogsheads. "To protect the hogshead," penned Brissot, "they put a couple of heavy hoops around it to roll it on…. [T]he price paid for this tobacco is lower than that paid for tobacco packed in hogsheads and transported in wagons."

Whether rolled, floated downstream on batteaux, or driven to market via wagons, Virginia tobacco found eager, addicted consumers all across western Europe. And Albemarle planters, like their Tidewater antecedents, dreamt that the noxious cash crop would eventually afford them more land, more slaves, and a life of luxury. But because tobacco drained the soil of valuable nutrients—notably nitrogen—it normally could be grown for only three years in the same field. Keeping up production, then, meant the constant clearing and cultivation of new land. Although many other staples were harvested in the county, and despite the arguments over its abuse of the soil, tobacco remained Albemarle's dominant agricultural product for most of a century.

With the 1761 partitioning of Albemarle, the county courthouse—at Scottsville on the James—was left at the southernmost section of the jurisdiction. This simply would not do.

continued Woods, "it lies in the midst of a fertile country, and it is beautiful for situation…. A thousand acres were purchased from Col. Richard Randolph, of Henrico, extending north and south from near Cochran's Pond to the south side of Moore's Creek, and east and west from the [old train depot in today's downtown] to Preston Heights [north of the University of Virginia]. The title to this property was vested in Dr. Thomas Walker as Trustee, and he was empowered to sell and convey it to purchasers. The town was planned at the eastern edge of this tract, and consisted of four tiers of squares—each tier running east and west, and containing seven squares—and the four tiers extending from Jefferson Street to the north to South Street on the south. The public square for the courthouse was exterior to the limits of the town."

With the county government set up, lucrative agriculture underway—and the region's two principal towns well-established and growing—the loyal citizens of Albemarle were looking forward to a prosperous and peaceful future.

Accordingly, an act of Assembly establishing the town of Charlottesville was passed in November of 1762. "Dictated by the spirit of loyalty then prevalent," wrote Woods, "the name was given in honor of Princess Charlotte of Mecklenburg Strelitz, who had recently become Queen of England as the wife of King George III."

Charlottesville's location was well-chosen. "It occupies almost the exact center of the county,"

❖

Top, left: Silhouette of Dr. Thomas Walker.

Top, right: Blenheim on the estate of John Carter, secretary of the colony.

Bottom, left: Albemarle County courthouse. The rear wing (on the right) was built in 1803 on the site of the original log structure. The front section was completed just prior to the Civil War.

IMAGE COURTESY OF THE AUTHOR

Bottom, right: Castle Hill, the home of Dr. Thomas Walker.

CHAPTER III

ALBEMARLE IN THE AMERICAN REVOLUTION

Despite its remote location, Albemarle made its mark during the conflict thanks largely to the native son who penned the Declaration. As the war dragged on, the county hosted a prisoner-of-war camp housing thousands of enemy soldiers, and Charlottesville served briefly as the capital of Virginia.

❖

A. Jefferson called the Declaration "an expression of the American mind."

Although well-lit, the Virginia delegate's lodgings on the outskirts of Philadelphia—in the house owned by bricklayer Jacob Graff, located at 7th and Market Streets—posed several problems. The ceilings above the furnished sitting room and bedchamber were low and the bed too small for the Albemarle native's long, lanky frame. Additionally, the stable across the way, while convenient, attracted immense horseflies which in the oppressive June heat swarmed through his open windows and onto his portable lap desk. Many of the hungry pests attacked his calves through his flimsy silk stockings. Nonetheless—despite buzzing insects and cramped quarters—the Graff House provided the thirty-three-year-old with the quiet, and the distance from the other delegates, that he needed for the weighty task at hand.

Following Virginia delegate Richard Henry Lee's stirring June 7 resolution—which stated, in part, that "these United colonies are and of right ought to be free and independent states"—Congress had decided to postpone the important decision until July 1. In the meantime a committee was selected and given the task of preparing a declaration. Besides Thomas Jefferson, this council included John Adams, Benjamin Franklin, Roger Sherman, and Robert R. Livingston. Despite the inclusion of older, and already famous men, the committee unanimously pressed Jefferson to "undertake the draught" alone, as he later remembered. Bent over his recently made "writing-box"—and using as a guide his recently written draft for the Virginia Constitution—Thomas Jefferson labored on the new document between June 11 and June 28, 1776.

Why had the young legislator from a backwoods county of the Old Dominion been chosen to pen the Declaration of Independence? It seemed important for a Virginian "to appear at the head of this business," as Adams wrote over forty-five years later, because many of the other colonies were as yet lukewarm on the issue. Also, according to Adams, Jefferson was not "obnoxious, suspected, and unpopular"—as Adams was—and was regarded as a talented writer.

Talented indeed. "The literary excellence of the Declaration," noted biographer Dumas Malone, "is best attested by the fact that it has stood the test of time." Years later Jefferson laid out his purposes in authoring this most famous state paper of the American Republic: "Not to find out new principles, or new arguments…but to place before mankind the common sense of the subject, in terms so plain and firm as to command their assent, and to justify ourselves in the independent stand we are compelled to take. Neither aiming at originality of principle or sentiment…it was intended to be an expression of the American mind…."

Across the colonies the "American mind" had already been expressing itself—since April of

Left: Thomas Jefferson (1743-1826).

Below: The second version of Monticello, completed in 1809.

PAINTING BY MIKE TRIMPE, AUTHOR'S COLLECTION.

1775—through open hostility to the Crown. With the outbreak of the Revolution, wrote the Rev. Edgar Woods, "the people of Albemarle were deeply aroused. Their opposition to the obnoxious measures of the British government was prompt and strong. Upon the first mutterings of the storm, an independent company of volunteers was formed, and by spirited resolves they devoted themselves to the public welfare." Charles Lewis, of North Garden, was elected captain while Dr. George Gilmer and John Marks were made lieutenants.

On the night of April 20, 1775—one day after the actions at Lexington and Concord—Governor Dunmore of Virginia, fearing an uprising, seized the gunpowder and weaponry in the Williamsburg magazine. When news of this reached the Piedmont, eighteen of the Albemarle minutemen, under Lieutenant Gilmer, immediately set out for the colonial capital. "They returned home shortly thereafter," wrote Woods, "in the midst of the prevailing uncertainty." On July 11, 1775—less than three months later—Gilmer again set out for Williamsburg, this time at the head of twenty-seven militiamen. Obviously, "the cause of America" was strongly felt in Albemarle County.

At the Virginia Convention—which met on July 17—it was decided to divide up the colony for the purpose of raising troops. Of the sixteen

❖

Above: The Battle of Germantown.

Right: Gravestone of Lettitia Shelby in Maplewood Cemetery. Shelby was the mother of Kentucky's first governor, Isaac Shelby, who won renown during the Revolution for his participation in the wildly successful battle of King's Mountain, South Carolina, fought on October 7, 1780.

1829 at the age of sixty-seven.) Older brother William stated in 1832 that he had served an amazing nine, three-month tours of duty.

Aside from Jefferson, the Albemarle native who exerted the greatest influence over the course of the Revolution was, undoubtedly, George Rogers Clark. Born in 1752 just north of present-day Charlottesville, Clark compiled an astounding military record in the Trans-Allegheny west. "In the Kentucky, Ohio, and Illinois country," wrote historian Alan Williams, "the Revolution was a continuation of the long series of bloody battles, ambushes, and deceptions which the Indians and whites had been perpetuating against each other since…the early 1770s."

In 1776—with the support of Virginia Gov. Patrick Henry—George Rogers Clark began his campaign by securing Virginia's sovereignty over

districts delineated, Albemarle, Buckingham, Amherst, and East Augusta County comprised one, and were instructed to each supply companies for a Piedmont battalion to be commanded by Col. George Matthews (who later became governor of Georgia). Albemarle's Charles Lewis was listed as second-in-command. "This battalion [which included two Albemarle companies] was raised and went into camp November 11th, 1775, three miles from Rockfish Gap," wrote Woods, "and continued in training till December 6th." Slated for garrison duty on the frontier, this unit was later designated the 14th Virginia Regiment—with Charles Lewis as colonel—and, in September of 1778, was renamed the 10th Virginia.

Albemarle soldiers, in various units, fought in all of the war's important engagements including Trenton, Brandywine, Germantown, Saratoga, Monmouth, Savannah, Charleston, Camden, King's Mountain, Cowpens, Guilford Court House, Eutaw Springs, and Yorktown. Typical of these Albemarle stalwarts—who most often served a great distance from the familiar, and comforting, Blue Ridge—were brothers Henry and William Carter. Henry (in September of 1779, when only seventeen) signed up for an eighteen-month stint in the 2nd Virginia Regiment under a Colonel Hawes. In that unit he faced the British regulars in four major southern-theater battles and was fairly lucky not to have caught a musket slug. (Based on his service Henry Carter applied for a pension in

Right: The Marquis de Lafayette.

*Below: Banastre Tarleton,
the Green Dragoon.*

the Kentucky area. Two years later, with only 175 well-armed backwoodsmen, Clark swept through the Illinois country capturing the British-held settlements of Kaskaskia, Cahokia, and Vincennes. The taking of Fort Sackville, at Vincennes in present-day Indiana, Williams called "the most remarkable single military feat of the Revolution." After wading through icy waters on low rations, Clark and his frontiersmen surrounded the fort and compelled its surrender after firing only a few well-placed shots. With but a small force this "Conqueror of the Northwest" had virtually guaranteed that Indiana, Illinois, Michigan, and Wisconsin would forevermore fly the Star and Stripes.

In the winter of 1778–1779 Albemarle County became home for thousands of hungry, weary foreigners. These were the soldiers of the "Convention Army," the British and Hessian force commanded by Gen. John "Gentleman Johnny" Burgoyne which he had surrendered at Saratoga, New York, fifteen months earlier and over 600 miles away. After being quartered around Boston for over a year, these prisoners were marched to the Virginia Piedmont—away from the active theater of war—during the final months of 1778.

Cold and famished, the 3,750-man Convention Army stumbled into Charlottesville in mid-January, 1779. "[N]o pen can describe the scene of misery and confusion that ensued," wrote Britisher Thomas Anbury of his arrival.

"[T]his famous place we had heard so much of," continued Anbury, a lieutenant in the 24th Regiment of Foot, "consisted only of a Courthouse, one tavern, and about a dozen houses; all of which were [already] crowded…. As to the men, the situation was truly horrible…they were, instead of comfortable barracks, conducted into a wood [approximately four miles northwest of Charlottesville], where a few log huts were just begun…the most part not covered over, and all of them full of snow; these the men were obliged to clear out, and cover over to secure themselves from the inclemency of the weather…." What made matters worse was the want of provisions. For six days Anbury and his fellow prisoners subsisted on "the meal of Indian corn made into cakes."

While the men and the junior officers made the best of their straits, the general officers moved into the area's better homes. British Maj. Gen. William Phillips occupied Blenheim, the Carter residence, while German Gen. Friedrich Adolph, Baron von Riedesel and his family and staff rented Colle in today's Simeon. Thomas Jefferson—who was governor for two one-year terms beginning in June of 1779—enjoyed entertaining von Riedesel and his well-educated aides at nearby Monticello.

With time, and no small amount of backbreaking work, the prisoner-of-war camp became habitable. Once the huts were roofed over the conventioners began clearing roads and

paths. Many planted and tended kitchen gardens, some raised chickens. Numerous springs provided fresh water for the parched foreigners; within a few months regular shipments of food began arriving. To help fill the long, idle hours the men erected churches and theaters.

Albemarle County went through quite a lot to maintain the soldiers. Trees were eventually cut down within a radius of six miles to provide firewood. The heavy demand for food caused prices to shoot up, and some locals feared starvation. The greatest fear, however, was that the Convention Army—the largest concentration of humanity in central Virginia—would overthrow its guards. The swarm of prisoners had been herded to Charlottesville under the watchful eye of two troops, or about fifty men, of Col. Theodoric Bland's 1st Regiment of Continental Light Dragoons—which looked, to Anburey, "as if the gibbets had been robbed to make it up...." This small cavalry guard, upon arrival, was immediately supplemented with the Albemarle Battalion, a 600-man Continental unit liable for service only within the borders of the county.

As its captivity dragged on, the Convention Army's numbers dwindled. Of the 3,750 who arrived in Albemarle—more than half of whom were British—fewer than 3,000 answered the roll in May of 1780. Most of those missing, no doubt, were escapees, men who had simply walked off

into the wilderness. Many of the Hessians who slipped away eventually took American wives and settled the fertile countryside.

Amazing as it may seem—and despite the presence of thousands of enemy prisoners—Albemarle County escaped the attentions of the British Army throughout the first five years of war. That was about to change. In October of 1780, after a large English force briefly occupied Portsmouth, Virginia, Governor Jefferson concluded that the Convention Army should be moved elsewhere. By the end of the year the prisoners who remained—a mere 2,000—were escorted away to points north. The decision proved fortuitous.

Events moved quickly in 1781. On January 5, a British raiding force under the despised traitor Benedict Arnold sailed up the James and took possession of Richmond, the new state capital. After destroying precious military stores, Arnold retired downriver to a fortified position. On May 20 he was joined by Gen. Charles Cornwallis, who had marched his veteran army up from North Carolina. Lord Cornwallis took command. British forces in Virginia now totaled 7,200. Facing them was the young Marquis de Lafayette with less than half that number, most of them militiamen. By judiciously retreating whenever threatened, the twenty-four-year-old Frenchman was able to keep his outmatched army intact.

Interestingly enough, the state government chose that same strategy. On May 10 the General Assembly had determined to quit Richmond—and skedaddle westward—because of the rapidly deteriorating military situation. It wasn't until May 28 that a quorum of legislators established themselves in the taverns adjacent to the court-

Above: Silhouette of Jack Jouett.

Left: Jouett's ride has been likened to that of Paul Revere.

Sketch of the old building at The Farm. It was here-and not under an oak tree-that Tarleton established his headquarters.

leaving behind his home, his position as chief executive of the state, and perhaps what little dignity remained to him as a public figure.

As the sun came up on June 4, Tarleton's dragoons galloped over Pantops Mountain, dispersed the militiamen defending the Rivanna crossing, and thundered onto the streets of tiny Charlottesville. But the game had scattered. "Such terror and confusion you have no idea of," wrote the daughter of Jacquelin Ambler, a member of Jefferson's council, "Governor, Council, everybody scampering." Forewarned, most of the legislators had made good their escape, riding frantically over the Blue Ridge to Staunton.

Nonetheless, Tarleton managed to nab a few, including Daniel Boone, a new member of the House of Delegates representing the huge, western county known as Kentucky. In the commotion around the courthouse Boone was apprehended when an alert British officer heard Jack Jouett refer to him as "captain." The scruffy frontiersman was tossed into a coal house for safe keeping. Hustled before Tarleton the next morning, Boone explained away his rank by claiming he had held it in Lord Dunmore's pre-Revolutionary militia. Tarleton released him.

When the excitement of the chase wore off, the enemy horsemen set about demolishing rebel property. They destroyed some Continental clothing, 400 barrels of powder, several hogsheads of tobacco and, as Tarleton later reported, broke up "1,000 new firelocks that had been manufactured at Fredericksburg...." Tarleton remained in Charlottesville—headquartered at "the Farm" just downhill from the courthouse—for one day, until June 5. When the enemy cavalrymen rode eastward to rejoin Cornwallis, the people of Albemarle were elated.

Lord Cornwallis surrendered at Yorktown a little over four months later—on October 19, 1781—thus effectively ending the war. The Revolutionary experience was over for Charlottesville and Albemarle County, but not for Thomas Jefferson. For years his political opponents played up his ineptitude as a wartime governor and his hurried retreat from Tarleton's dragoons. Indeed, the thirty-eight-year-old Jefferson marked his governorship as the very nadir of his political career. Little did he realize that his years of public service had only just begun.

house at Charlottesville, the new capital. "Retiring before the enemy the government of the proud Commonwealth of Virginia not only lost all semblance of impressiveness," wrote Henry "Light Horse Harry" Lee. "In the process of transferring its seat…it practically dissolved."

On June 3, Lord Cornwallis unleashed two large cavalry forces to slash into the interior of the state—the most famous of these, under Lieut. Col. Banastre Tarleton, to "disturb the Assembly then sitting at Charlottesville and to destroy the stores there…." The possible capture of Governor Jefferson, author of the seditious Declaration, must certainly have spurred Tarleton—regarded as "the very model of a partisan leader"—to even greater-than-normal celerity. (Coincidently, Jefferson's second one-year term as governor ended on June 3, the very day Tarleton set off.)

Tarleton—with a mounted force of 250—rode hard toward Charlottesville and his prey, seventy miles to the west. In passing through Louisa County, however, the green-jacketed raiders caught the attention of John "Jack" Jouett, a captain in the state militia. Realizing Tarleton's objective, the twenty-seven-year-old patriot—thanks to his thoroughbred, his familiarity with the back roads, and a brilliant full moon—covered the distance overnight, arriving in time to warn Jefferson at Monticello as well as the assemblymen just then enjoying their morning cups. Jefferson, after first sending his family off to Blenheim, packed up his most important papers then—at the very last possible moment—rode up over Carter's Mountain to safety. He was

CHAPTER IV

JEFFERSON, ALBEMARLE'S FAVORITE NATIVE SON

Born in 1743, Thomas Jefferson rose to the heights of fame for his Declaration,
and his many years spent in public service. Nonetheless, despite the time spent away from Monticello,
Jefferson made many contributions to his native region. The intellectuals who visited "the Sage of Monticello"
helped introduce Albemarle to the nation, and the world.

Jefferson during his time as minister
to France. In this portrait his red hair
is hidden beneath a powdered wig.

Public service was a "raison d'être" for Thomas Jefferson. "If, in the course of my life, it has been in any degree useful to the cause of humanity," he wrote in 1815, "the fact itself bears its full reward." Throughout the ensuing years, humanity has countless times sized up his worth. Perhaps more than any other American of the Revolutionary generation, his was an existence filled with utility.

Education and hard work were the foundations of his many achievements. Born on April 13, 1743—at Shadwell, the home of his father, Peter Jefferson—Thomas Jefferson learned at an early age

❖

*Above: The entrance to Shadwell,
where the author of the Declaration
was born.*

*Right: Monticello's West Portico,
or garden entrance.*

Tuckahoe, a family plantation perched above the James River but a few miles west of Richmond. He read Greek and Latin under Reverends William Douglas and James Maury.

From 1760 until 1762 he studied at the College of William and Mary, an institution Dumas Malone called the continent's pre-eminent "school for statesmen." It was there, in Williamsburg, that Jefferson fell under the wonderful influence of mathematics professor William Small—"a man profound in most of the useful branches of science," he later wrote, "with a happy talent of communication...& an enlarged & liberal mind." There, too, he encountered George Wythe, perhaps the colonies' finest legal scholar. "Mr. Wythe continued to be my faithful and beloved Mentor in youth," noted Jefferson in his Autobiography. "In 1767, he led me into the practice of the law...at which I continued until the revolution shut up the courts of justice."

In 1769 Jefferson was elected by Albemarle's freeholders as one of their two representatives in the House of Burgesses, the colonial legislature. Only twenty-five at the time, he continued as a member of that body until 1775. His authorship of the Declaration of Independence the following year brought him both worldwide renown and a measure of appreciation from his fellow

to apply himself rigorously to every task at hand. He began his studies at an "English School" at

citizens that would be very difficult to exaggerate. While serving in the new Virginia State Legislature (1776 to 1779) Jefferson laid the groundwork for the eventual reform of the Old Dominion's ancient, indeed feudal, land inheritance laws. He also established for Virginians the beginnings of a public school system and complete religious freedom. "As a result," noted Malone, Jefferson began "to appear on the page of history as a major prophet of intellectual liberty and human enlightenment."

Jefferson's two years as a wartime Virginia governor were, as previously noted, fraught with controversy and disappointment. In 1783, following the end of the Revolution, he wrote the draft for Virginia's constitution and was briefly a member of the Continental Congress. Jefferson served as minister to France from 1785 to 1789, then as our nation's first secretary of state from 1790 to 1793. As vice president under John Adams (1797 to 1801), Jefferson penned the Kentucky Resolutions, one of the first delineations of States' Rights theory.

Elected third president of the United States in March of 1801—following a painfully long deadlock with Aaron Burr in the House of Representatives—Jefferson was the first chief executive inaugurated in Washington, a city he had helped plan. During his two-term presidency, the Jefferson administration orchestrated the purchase of Louisiana from Napoleon—thus virtually doubling the country's size—and dispatched the Meriwether Lewis and William Clark Expedition, along with several others, to officially take its measure.

After his eight years as president Jefferson returned home to his beloved Monticello, his mountaintop home. During his seventeen-year retirement he continued to make his mark on his native region. There's no doubting that in Albemarle County Jefferson's footprints were— and remain to this day—indelible.

The first impression had been made in 1765. Tobacco was central Virginia's first cash crop. As it grew in prominence, the need arose for organized transportation. The "noxious weed" had to be delivered to market and the luxuries of civilization had to be hauled into the interior. In October of 1765, the General Assembly passed an act "for clearing the great falls of James river [at Richmond]…and the north branch of James

river"—the Rivanna. In the group of trustees established to receive subscriptions for the Rivanna River was the twenty-two-year-old Thomas Jefferson, "the initiator of the project," according to Malone, "and probably the most active member."

Two hundred pounds were raised to make improvements on Albemarle's waterway. The river was surveyed and the channel eventually perfected by dredging and removing trees and large rocks. Proudly Jefferson later listed the endeavor as his first "service" to the public. In the 1780s—in his *Notes on the State of Virginia*—he described the Rivanna as "navigable for canoes and batteaux to its intersection with the South West Mountains, which is about 22 miles."

Local titles came early in life for Thomas Jefferson. In 1770—one year after his election to the House of Burgesses—the Royal governor of Virginia, Lord Botetourt, named Jefferson lieutenant of Albemarle County, overall head of the local militia. "Thus, at the age of twenty-seven," noted Malone, "he became the ranking official of his County and could be called Colonel. His service in this important post may not have been continuous, but he was occupying it when war actually broke out…." Seven years later Colonel Jefferson was named an Albemarle magistrate.

Jefferson's interest in agriculture greatly benefited the county. Filippo Mazzei—an Italian entrepreneur of the first order—arrived in

❖

Above: Formally authorized in 1827, the Rivanna Navigation Company continued the work begun by Jefferson.

Below: Engraving of Monticello's East Portico. From "A Map of Albemarle County, Va." by G. Peyton.

Williamsburg in November of 1773. Thanks to the efforts of Thomas Adams, a wealthy merchant, the Virginia Legislature had promised Mazzei 5,000 acres in Augusta County for the express purpose of establishing vineyards. Mazzei and his laborers stayed briefly at the home of Francis Eppes, Thomas Jefferson's brother-in-law, then set out for the Shenandoah Valley together with Adams. "It was unfortunate for these plans," wrote Malone, "that they stopped for an evening at Monticello."

The next morning, as was his custom, the thirty-year-old Thomas Jefferson arose early. Excited about hosting a European visitor, Jefferson took Mazzei on one of his long rambles about the neighborhood. It was decided in a twinkling. The southeastern slopes of Monticello, an estate called Colle, seemed perfect for the Italian's vines. Plus, as Jefferson had surplus land, remembered Mazzei, "he made me a gift of a tract of 2,000 acres." Within a short time a dozen other Italians arrived, "and to their delight the tall, friendly Virginian," wrote Malone, "talked with them in Tuscan, which he had picked up unaided. Thus did Jefferson help introduce Italian wines and vegetables into the red-clay country, and with them new varieties of spades and billhooks...."

Improvements to the Monticello plantation, made at various times, were also of benefit to local residents. Peter Jefferson had built a mill at Shadwell in 1757, "drawing the water," noted Thomas Jefferson Wertenbaker, "by means of a canal from a dam a half-mile up stream." Everything was swept away by the great freshet of 1771. After the Revolution Thomas Jefferson built at Shadwell, continued Wertenbaker, "a toll mill for the grinding of his own and his neighbors' grain, a sawmill, and a manufacturing flour mill. The last named was sixty feet by forty, was three stories high, and cost $1,000." The flour produced was stuffed into hogsheads, rolled onto batteaux, and floated to market in Richmond.

In 1810 Jefferson wrote to the Rivanna Navigation Company (which had been set up to further improve the river): "Your gentlemen directors…desire the use of my dam to keep back water at its present navigable state. Use it…. You also wish to use my canal. You are welcome to it." With this letter Jefferson also granted the enterprise the right to widen his canal, and gave it—free of charge—the site on which to construct a lock, as well as the "timber, earth, and stone to build it."

Of the approximately 5,500 acres Jefferson owned in Albemarle only about one-fifth were ever under cultivation. Sometime in the 1790s he had begun devoting much of this acreage to wheat. Although he employed a system of rotation, even this cash crop was insufficient to support him. "In searching for supplemental income," wrote biographer Noble E. Cunningham, Jr., "Jefferson set up a shop to manufacture nails at Monticello, employing a dozen slave boys, aged ten to sixteen, and supervising the details of the business himself." By 1796 the Monticello nailery was producing one ton of nails per month.

The limited income from farming also encouraged Jefferson, wrote Cunningham, "to increase crop production by better organization of his labor force and greater use of labor-saving devices." He developed, for example, a "mold-board plow of least resistance" and tested it on his property. "He continued to perfect his invention," noted Cunningham, "and in time his improvement attracted considerable attention from scientists and agriculturalists…. Jefferson also directed the building of a threshing machine at Monticello from a model sent to him from England…. He built the horse-powered works compact enough to be portable from field to field on a wagon and first used it in the harvest of 1796."

During this same period—as wrote William F. and George R. Minor, contributors to *The Magazine of Albemarle County History*—"a number of planters in the Albemarle County area initiated agricultural reforms on lands which had been depleted by tobacco production, poor farming methods, and erosion." Two decades later—on May 5, 1817—about thirty of these landowners founded the Agricultural Society of Albemarle, with Jefferson, naturally, as one of its leaders. In 1819 John S. Skinner's *American Farmer*, printed in Baltimore, became the journal of record for the organization's experiments and papers. "This society," noted the brothers Minor, "would have considerable influence during the ensuing years."

Architecture was one of Jefferson's greatest fascinations. "In his own developing region

❖

Above, left: Jefferson's Cabinet, or office, at Monticello. Note (at the center): his copying machine (a model 1806 Hawkins & Peale Polygraph), and revolving bookstand. The busts (left to right) are of: John Adams, George Washington, and Jefferson.

Above, right: A bust of Benjamin Franklin looks down over Monticello's sun-drenched Tea Room.

Below: In the Parlor at Monticello— the 1789 Houdon bust of 46-year-old Jefferson, a chess set, and the gorgeous parquet floor.
IMAGES COURTESY OF BRUCE YOUNG.

Jefferson became notable for his knowledge of the arts," wrote Malone, "but his consuming interest in architecture began, not with his concern for culture, but with his desire to engage in actual construction, or to help his friends do so."

Monticello—Italian for "little mountain"—is Jefferson's finest architectural legacy. (His design of the University of Virginia's original structures is discussed in Chapter VI.) It was the epicenter of his life, especially so during the ex-president's seventeen-year retirement in Albemarle County. "I am as happy nowhere else, and in no other society," he wrote, "and all my wishes end, where I hope my days will, at Monticello."

A self-taught architect, Jefferson labored for forty years on his hilltop villa (from 1769 to 1809) and succeeded in creating, but two miles southeast of Charlottesville, a beautiful homage to antiquity, one of the nation's first neo-classical homes. In its conception Jefferson relied heavily on the published works of Andrea Palladio, a sixteenth-century Italian who had carefully measured, and illustrated, the structural remains of the ancient world. Monticello's interior, wrote Jefferson, "contains specimens of all of the different orders…. The [Entrance] Hall is in the Ionic, the Dining Room is in the Doric, the Parlor is in the Corinthian, and the Dome in the Attic."

The rooms on Monticello's main floor were also brimming with art, artifacts, and curios. The eighteen-foot-high walls of the entrance hall, for example, were covered with maps of Virginia and the world's continents. Cartography was yet another of his many passions. The room also featured dozens of Native American items sent back by Lewis and Clark, and the massive bones of an American Mastodon, a pre-historic elephant, which had been unearthed for Jefferson at Big Bone Lick, Kentucky in 1807.

His art collection was scattered throughout. In the tea room sat his "most honourable suite," terra-cotta busts of John Paul Jones, Benjamin Franklin, George Washington, and the Marquis de Lafayette. A set of paintings related to the discovery of America—images of Amerigo Vespucci, Christopher Columbus, and Sir Walter Raleigh—hung in the parlor.

Jefferson was also quite the "gadgeteer." He was fascinated by gadgets and had several installed at Monticello after first encountering, and inspecting, their prototypes in other gentlemen's homes. These delightful devices included a revolving serving door and a pair of wine-bottle dumbwaiters, like little elevators, used to hoist Madeira and other varietals up from the wine cellar below. In his office he employed a copying machine—a Hawkins and Peale Polygraph—to duplicate thousands of his letters. He called it "the finest invention of the present age."

His age—and, indeed, humanity itself—were made much the richer thanks to Jefferson's dedicated and well-lived life. Visitors to the "little mountain" typically departed dazzled by the eclectic home and its distinguished master. "Mr. Jefferson"—wrote the chevalier de Chastellux, a member of the French Academy, in 1782—"is the first American who has consulted the Fine Arts to know how he should shelter himself from the weather." Fourteen years later Irishman Isaac Weld called Monticello "one of the most elegant private habitations in the United States." Bostonian George Ticknor wrote of "the strange furniture of its walls."

These men made the pilgrimage to Monticello to meet the brilliant intellectual who had first dreamed of it, as well as of our free nation, while the American colonies were still beneath a Royal heel. "Today's visitor," wrote historian Merrill Peterson, "may have his encounter with that genius extended and enhanced by placing himself imaginatively in the long train of thoughtful journeyers who have gone before him."

Top: Jefferson as he appeared during his early retirement.

Below: The headstone of Benjamin Franklin Ficklin who owned Monticello during the last year of the Civil War. A native of Albemarle County, Ficklin was one of the founders of the Pony Express and operated blockade runners during the conflict.

IMAGE COURTESY OF THE AUTHOR

CHAPTER V

YEARS OF PROSPERITY:

ALBEMARLE FROM THE 1780s TO THE 1820s

*After the Revolution the county grew in population and wealth. More churches were built
and more villages established. Wheat replaced tobacco as the area's principal product and the riverside towns
of Scottsville and Milton connected Albemarle to the mighty James and markets to the east.*

Following the end of the American Revolution Albemarle had embarked on a period of prosperity. The conflict had pushed the frontier to the west, to Kentucky and beyond. "Albemarle County no longer could be considered part of that nebulous line of scattered settlement," wrote historian John Hammond Moore, "it was becoming, in fact, an established community which, in time, would serve as a center of business and commercial activity."

❖

*Charles Keck's fabulous Meriwether
Lewis and William Clark statue—at
the intersection of West Main and
Ridge-McIntire streets—also includes
Sacajawea, their Shoshone guide.*
IMAGE COURTESY OF THE AUTHOR

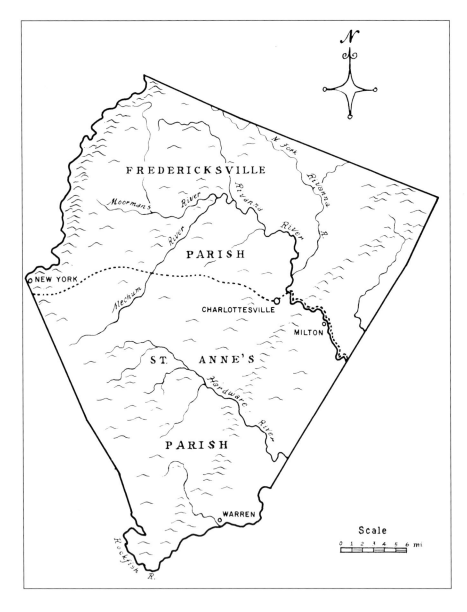

Map illustrated by John
Middleton Freeman.

Peace and prosperity are great inducements to population growth. In 1790, the first federal census counted 12,585 souls in the county: 6,835 whites and 5,750 blacks, of which number only 171 were freemen. Ten years later—at the dawning of a new century—Albemarle County boasted 4,000 more citizens. Charlottesville, too, was growing. In 1779, for example, prisoner-of-war Anburey had noted that the village contained "about a dozen houses." But three years later the chevalier de Chastellux called it "a rising little town."

By the first decade of the nineteenth century it was obvious to all that Albemarle was on the upswing. Virginia visitor Sir Augustus John Foster called the county "a rather populous district." Journeying alongside the Southwest Mountains in 1808, he "passed a very pretty wooden house with a portico...as well as several other settlements—as farm houses on a large

scale are called in these parts—on either side of the road.... [Albemarle] is on the great high road to New Orleans, to which the mail was carried in twenty days from Washington...." Writing at about the same time, New Yorker John Edwards Caldwell commented on the beauty of Farmington, west of Charlottesville. In the village's outlying regions, he wrote, there "are some handsome farms and elegant houses, the spacious and well appointed mansion and ground of Mr. [George] Divers, are well worth notice."

Indeed there were many things worthy of notice in Albemarle during this period—one was that the time had arrived for the establishment of more towns. Charlottesville, it will be remembered, had been laid out in 1762, but initially its growth was very slow. Warren—at the mouth of Ballinger Creek—was created in 1789. Other towns soon followed. "Private speculations," noted guidebook writer Eudora Ramsey Richardson, "brought into temporary being Travellers Grove, New York—colloquially known as 'Little York'—Morgantown, and Barterbrook."

Scottsville, on the James River—at the place where the first Albemarle courthouse had its brief but important existence—was incorporated as a town in 1818. Although the county's seat of justice had already been moved to Charlottesville—a point of contention—Scottsville, according to Rev. Edgar Woods, "continued nevertheless to be a place of considerable notoriety." Originally created on fifteen acres of John Scott's land—subdivided into half-acre lots—additional property was attached later to its western boundary. "In 1824 the Staunton and James River Turnpike was commenced," noted Woods, "and Scottsville was its river terminus. Because of its fine shipping facilities, it was not long before great numbers of huge wagons thronged its streets...and it became the emporium of a busy commerce."

The advantages of transporting goods via the Rivanna River had also given birth to another town—Milton. It was located along the right bank of the river, approximately four miles downstream, or east, of its junction with Moore's Creek. Here the Rivanna—after rushing through the Southwest Mountains—scribes a long curve to the northeast. Three Notched Road, winding its way west to the misty Blue Ridge, lay to the north only a half mile distant.

Bennett Henderson, a local magistrate, had been the first to see promise in the river's fertile bend. Sometime in the mid-1700s, he had erected there a large flouring mill, a good-sized tobacco warehouse, and more importantly, a wharf along the riverbank. "Henderson's" was born. Within time Thomas Jefferson, as previously mentioned, built his mills nearby.

Soon business began to pick up, and a steady stream of fifty-foot-long batteaux, or tobacco boats, were plying the Rivanna down to the James. Thanks to Henderson's proximity to the well-traveled Three Notched Road, farmers from all across the central Piedmont started hauling their tobacco to his wharf for transshipment. "In 1789," wrote historian Geoffrey B. Henry, "Henderson's warehouse was designated one of two official tobacco inspection stations in Albemarle County." That same year the General Assembly, in responce to numerous petitions, officially turned "Henderson's" into "Milton."

The 1790s were Milton's boom years. Aside from being the head of navigation on the Rivanna, it quickly became, according to Woods, "the shipping port of perhaps three-fourths of the county, and of a large section of the Shenandoah Valley." By 1794 Milton had its own free ferry, and, four years later, its own post office. At the turn of the century the village contained close to two-dozen structures.

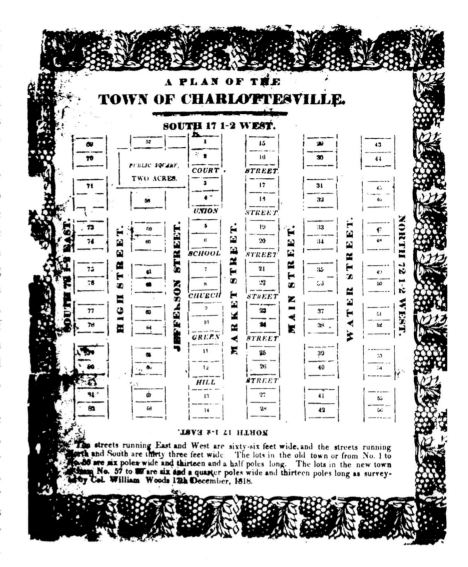

❖

Above: Plan of Charlottesville, 1818.

Left: Farmington, the home of George Divers. The octagonal entrance hall, pictured here, was designed by President Jefferson in 1802. It was completed fifty years later.

Milton's heyday, however, was relatively short-lived. The often unpredictable waters of the Rivanna were both its lifeblood and its poison. As early as 1812, for example, the river had been "improved" upstream—past Milton—as far as Moore's Ford near Charlottesville. With more riverine improvements Charlottesville continued growing as a shipping center while Milton declined. Another dunking was delivered by competition from Scottsville. When that town's riverside facilities were enlarged it could rightly boast of being Albemarle's biggest port. Soon more produce was being hauled in wagons to Scottsville than was being loaded into batteaux at Milton. As business dwindled so did its population. Milton's last gasp for air could barely be heard above the 1870 torrent that carried away what was left of its old mills and warehouses.

In the final decades of the eighteenth century Albemarle was becoming civilized, and a civilized people require religion. The county's first religious gatherings, wrote local historian Mary Rawlings, "were held in private homes, until the increase in population made possible the erection of small and plain church buildings, usually of wood." Prior to the Revolution the Church of England—the Anglican faith—had been the established religion throughout the colony. Supported by public levies, or tithes, each parish—Fredericksville above the Three Notched Road and St. Anne's below—exercised

both religious and civil power through its vestry. "Vestrymen, usually wealthy citizens who often viewed their duties as an important step on the path to political success," noted Moore, "were charged with care of the poor, orphans, and mentally deficient." Following disestablishment these important duties were undertaken by "overseers of the poor."

Religious life in Albemarle was concentrated in the countryside. Indeed, as late as the mid-1820s there was not a house of worship in Charlottesville. "To some extent," wrote Moore, "this situation was a reflection of the disarray Anglicans experienced during the early decades of independence and a general agnosticism prevalent among intellectuals which, at times, bordered on atheism."

Nonetheless, the county contained a large number of the faithful. The Baptists had started their career in Albemarle in 1773, at a meeting house built on the land of David Lewis just west of Charlottesville. Their first pastor was Andrew Tribble. By 1809, Albemarle held five Baptist churches. The first local Methodist church was built at Whitehall in 1788. Since the earliest days of settlement Presbyterians had abounded in Albemarle's western reaches.

Eventually, of course, religion made its way into the settlements, despite the lack of tabernacles. "In our village of Charlottesville," wrote Thomas Jefferson in 1822, "there is a good degree of religion, with a small spice only of fanaticism. We have four sects, but without either church or meeting house. The court is the common temple, one Sunday in the month to each. Here, Episcopalian and Presbyterian, Methodist and Baptist, meet together, join in hymning their Maker, listen with attention and devotion to each others' preachers, and all mix in society in perfect harmony."

The ideal of perfect harmony among people was closely intertwined with another of Jefferson's—that of an agrarian-based society. "Cultivators of the earth are the most valuable citizens," he had written in 1785. "They are the most vigorous, the most independent, the most virtuous, and they are tied to their country and wedded to its liberty and interest, by the most lasting bonds." It was this overriding interest in things agrarian that led to his efforts toward switching Albemarle's cash crop from tobacco to wheat. Tobacco, everyone knew, was simply ruining the soil. Visitors often noticed the county's many abandoned fields, the red-clay hillsides eaten away by gullies and washouts.

In Albemarle the transformation to a wheat economy began sometime in the 1790s. Jefferson, it appears, turned away from tobacco cultivation around the middle of the decade. "The small farmers often followed the example of their wealthier neighbors," wrote William Minor Dabney. "Travelers found that in 1796 the shift away from tobacco was almost complete." In general, penned Moore, "the expanding fields of grain bestowed a measure of prosperity upon Albemarle County."

Not to mention a splendor so sublime that it captured the imagination of popular writer George Bagby. "The forest once passed," he wrote, "a scene not of enchantment...but of exceeding beauty, met the eye. Wide, very wide fields of waving grain, billowing seas of green and gold, as the season chanced to be, over which the scudding shadows chased and played, gladdened the heart with wealth far spread.... Beneath the tree-clumps, fat cattle chewed the cud or peaceful sheep reposed, grateful for the shade.... Seen by the tired horseman, halting at the woodland's edge, this picture, steeped in the intense, quivering summer

noonlight, filled the soul with unspeakable emotions of beauty, tenderness, peace, *home.*"

In the first decade of the nineteenth century Albemarle was gratified to learn that another of its native sons had greatly benefited the nation. Born at Locust Hill, near Ivy Depot—on August 18, 1774—Meriwether Lewis had become an expert hunter at a very early age. "When he arrived at maturity," wrote Thomas Walker Gilmer, "his love of action led him into the regular army. He was the private secretary of

The 1859 wing of the county courthouse. It was built on the site of the original, whose grounds once featured the customary whipping post, stocks, and pillory.

IMAGE COURTESY OF THE AUTHOR

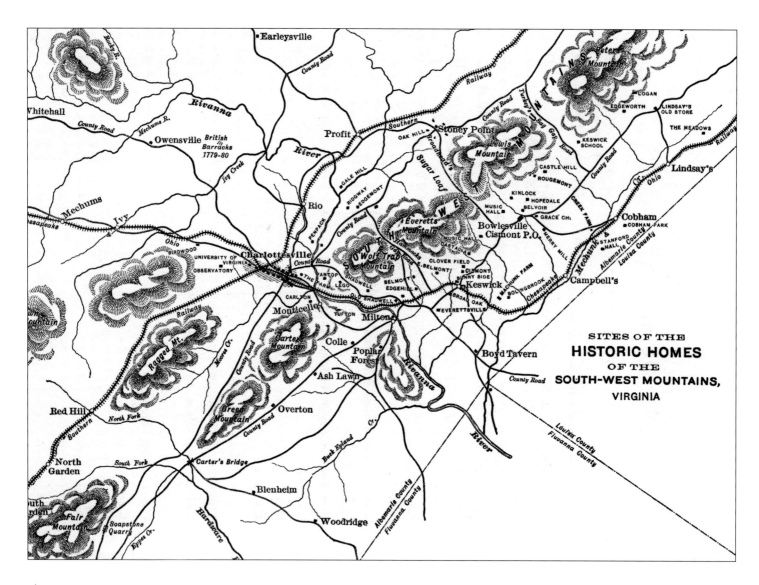

Many of Albemarle's historic homes sit to the east of the Southwest Mountains.

President Jefferson when the government determined to have the territory of Louisiana explored…. His known intrepidity and perseverance pointed him out as the fittest person to head an expedition for that purpose. He selected for his aid and companion his friend [William] Clark of the army."

Lewis and Clark, and their forty-five-man Corps of Discovery, set out from St. Louis, upstream on the Missouri River, in May of 1804. After tremendous suffering they succeeded in crossing the continental divide and followed the Columbia River to the Pacific Ocean. Their first sight of the great western water was on November 7, 1805. They wintered there and in March began their trek back. Lewis and Clark returned to St. Louis—to great national acclaim—in September of 1806. They had performed the first recorded journey across the continent. In the process the Corps of Discovery had lost but one man.

The War of 1812, wrote Rawlings, "was a conflict in which the County must have felt a partisan concern, since James Madison and James Monroe, by virtue of office, were responsible for its declaration and conduct. Though Mr. Madison was never a resident of Albemarle, he was, from youth, intimately associated with its social and political life."

James Monroe had been born in Westmoreland County—on Virginia's Northern Neck—on April 28, 1758. A hero of the Battle of Trenton, the foundation of Monroe's political career was the close friendship that had resulted from his studying the law (from 1780 to 1783) under the tutelage of then-governor Thomas Jefferson. "In 1793 he bought and built on the east side of Carter's Mountain," wrote Rawlings, "calling his estate [Highland], and spending there the working years of his life. During this period he was three times Governor of Virginia, served as Minister to France and to England, and was twice President of the United States."

When war came, Monroe had been President Madison's secretary of state. In 1814 he also took on the duties of secretary of war. Fortunately, the contest affected only the Virginia Tidewater region (due to the British fleet's control of the Chesapeake). It never reached the Piedmont. Nonetheless, local men served with the army. A company of Virginia militia under Capt. Triplett T. Estes was raised in Albemarle. "A cavalry company from the county commanded by Colonel Samuel Carr," wrote Woods, "and an infantry company of which Achilles Broadhead was Captain, were also called into service."

At war's end Albemarle's prosperous country life resumed. "The society in Albemarle is much better than is common in country situations," wrote Jefferson in 1815 to a European correspondent. "Perhaps there is not a better country society in the United States. But do not imagine that this is a Parisian or an academical society." Thanks to the efforts of the ex-president that was about to change.

CHAPTER VI

THE UNIVERSITY OF VIRGINIA:

THE "HOBBY" OF JEFFERSON'S OLD AGE

Not content to retire quietly, Thomas Jefferson founded the University and served as its first rector.
The Marquis de Lafayette was wined and dined in the Rotunda in 1824. Within but a few years of opening,
the University of Virginia became one of the South's most prominent schools.

The University Lawn, looking north.

IMAGE COURTESY OF THE AUTHOR.

Albemarle County had never seen the like. Hundreds of people lined the dusty roadway leading west from the little town of Charlottesville. The noisy throng included shop-owners, slaves, and several tottering veterans of the American Revolution. That day—it was November 5, 1824—they had buttoned on their ragged, ancient coatees in honor of the general they had not seen in over forty years. When the cavalcade finally approached the old soldiers saluted—the civilians cheered. "It was love," reported Fredericksburg's *Virginia Herald*, "it was the brazen memory of his services, and sacrifices for us that swelled the hearts and glistened in the eyes of the people."

Leading the parade—astride a large, prancing charger—rode the event's "chief marshal" accompanied by his aides. Behind them rolled the center of attention—a magnificent, jet-black landau—in which sat, according to the Charlottesville *Central Gazette*, "a hero of the revolution with two of its sages": the Marquis de Lafayette accompanied by ex-presidents Thomas Jefferson and James Madison.

In the back of the carriage, Jefferson must have smiled proudly as his University of Virginia came suddenly into view. The structures were set off that day in a manner thoroughly unique. "Ranged aloft on the terraces," reported the *Virginia Herald*, "a thousand daughters of the mountains waved their white kerchiefs in the air. It was beautiful." Jefferson, of course, simply had to give Lafayette a tour of the project he fondly called the "hobby" of his old age.

Of Jefferson's many and varied accomplishments he asked that only three be inscribed on his tombstone—that he was the author of the Declaration of Independence, and of the Virginia Statute for Religious Freedom, and that he was father of the University of Virginia. Soon after opening its doors in 1825 his "academical village" became one of Virginia's—and indeed the South's—most important institutions of higher learning.

The founding of the University of Virginia was a process of many years, much sweat, and considerable debate. The school went through several phases in its development. In 1776, Thomas Jefferson—then a member of a committee tasked with restructuring the laws of Virginia—developed a comprehensive plan for general education. Though not adopted, the

plan—the dream—remained with him for the rest of his days.

U.Va.'s first incarnation took shape on January 12, 1803. On that date was formed Albemarle Academy, a secondary school for boys. Its fifteen trustees were granted authority to raise by subscription and lottery the $3,000 needed to begin construction. The records of further proceedings, if there were any, were lost and it is unclear whether the organization ever progressed beyond the planning stage.

Eleven years later—on March 25, 1814—five academy trustees met to appoint a new roster of thirteen, one of whom was ex-president Jefferson. About this time Jefferson wrote Peter Carr outlining his ideas for education in the Old Dominion. Often called "the most important document in the early history of the University," it describes three levels of schools—Elementary, General, and Professional—the classes of society most likely to benefit from them, and a complete

Above: Plaster lifemask of Thomas Jefferson executed in 1825 by John Bowere. Unfortunately, the plaster dried too quickly and had to be chiseled off.

Left: A view of Pavilion II from the Rotunda's South Portico.
IMAGE COURTESY OF THE AUTHOR

Above, left: Pavilions I and III of the West Lawn.

Above, right: Joseph Carrington Cabell, 1778-1856.

breakdown of three university-level departments: Languages, Mathematics, and Philosophy.

The sciences, wrote Jefferson, should be taught in the Professional Schools. In order for the students to master those subjects, he reasoned, they must first be offered in the General Schools. To accomplish these lofty goals, Jefferson suggested that Albemarle Academy be transformed into a higher-level institution. A petition was sent to the General Assembly and it was approved in February of 1816. The University of Virginia's second incarnation—Central College—was born. Funded by a liberal private subscription of up to $44,000, the project was also endowed by the state "with the proceeds from the sales of certain glebe lands and church property in the Parish of St. Anne."

Central College's first Board of Visitors included Jefferson, James Madison, James Monroe, Joseph Carrington Cabell, and John Hartwell Cocke. These last two were instrumental in the school's final metamorphosis. Cabell was a well-educated man, a state senator during the period when the plans for education were debated. He was a close friend of Jefferson, concurred with many of his views, and zealously backed the various educational bills the ex-president presented. John Hartwell Cocke was the owner of Bremo, a large estate on the James River near Scottsville. Well known throughout Virginia, Cocke had served as a general during the War of 1812, and was a well-spoken proponent of the colonization and temperance movements. To Jefferson's plans for education he gave liberally of his money and talents. Later, Cocke helped supervise the construction of some of U.Va.'s original buildings, including the Rotunda.

Jefferson went to work on Central College with a level of energy that belied his seventy-plus years. He performed all the tasks of a chief executive officer, and then some. He purchased the land, and surveyed and designed the grounds and buildings. Jefferson also fashioned its curriculum.

The cornerstone of the first structure—Pavilion VII—was laid during a ceremony in 1817.

A bill to set up a state university passed in 1818, but did not specify its location. Soon thereafter, a commission met at Rockfish Gap to decide between the cities of Staunton, Charlottesville, and Lexington. Thomas Jefferson and James Madison were both members. Proponents of Washington College in Lexington lobbied vigorously. As chairman, Jefferson naturally backed the location nearest his home, and nearest his heart. Of the three potential sites, moreover, Charlottesville was closer to the center of the Commonwealth. And several buildings at Central College were already under construction. After many hours of debate, the commission decided in favor of Charlottesville. The General Assembly granted the charter for the University of Virginia on January 25, 1819.

The Board of Visitors of the University of Virginia met for the first time two months later. Seated at the table were Thomas Jefferson, James Madison, Joseph Cabell, John Hartwell Cocke, Chapman Johnson, James Breckenridge, and Robert B. Taylor. Four of these men had been Visitors of Central College. They appointed the school's bursar, ordered a complete statement of property and funds, and set the compensation for professors. They also agreed that all available monies should be devoted to the buildings. The pace of construction on the ridge one mile west of Charlottesville took a noticeable step forward.

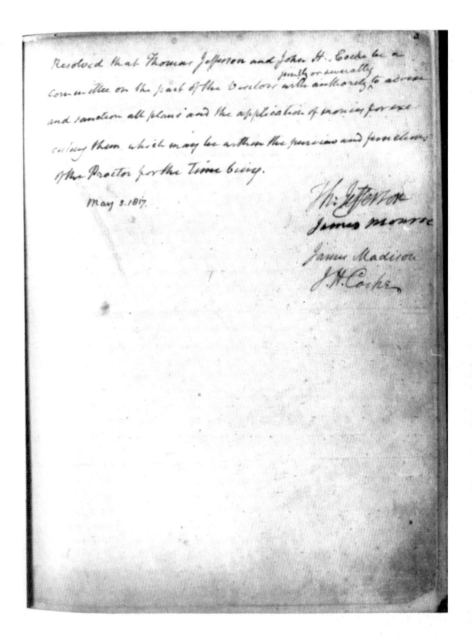

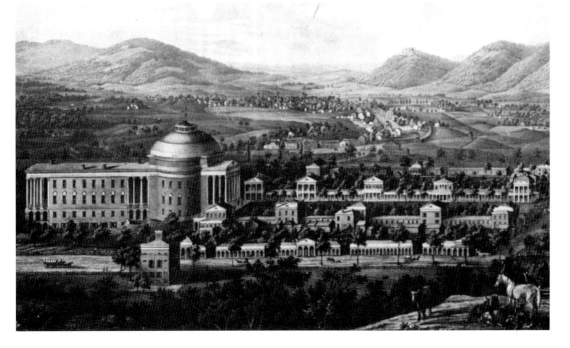

❖

Above: Minutes of the University's Board of Visitors showing the signatures of Jefferson, James Monroe, James Madison, and John Hartwell Cocke.

Left: The original Grounds viewed from the west. Note Monticello Mountain in the distance, just beyond Charlottesville.

Above, left: The Rotunda, completed in September of 1826.

IMAGE COURTESY OF THE AUTHOR.

Above, right: J. Robley Dunglison (1798-1869), the University's first professor of medicine and Jefferson's personal physician.

Jefferson had surveyed the original grounds in 1817 at the age of seventy-four. During the planning process he had requested suggestions from Benjamin Latrobe, an accomplished architect then working on the U.S. Capitol. An early Latrobe sketch shows a long, open quadrangle—or Lawn—flanked by student rooms and two-story buildings. One of the quadrangle's short sides was dominated by a large, circular building, or Rotunda.

The Lawn Jefferson adopted covers nearly two acres. Its rectangular layout takes advantage of a long, rocky ridge running south to north—its southern edge being the lowest. The Rotunda sits at its northern peak. The ridge's southward slope made it necessary to lay out the Lawn in three, fairly equal terraces. Each of the Lawn's long sides contains five, two-story Pavilions connected by student rooms set back behind rows of columns. Twenty-eight student rooms comprise the West Lawn with twenty-six opposite them on the East Lawn. The East and West Ranges—two more rows of student rooms—parallel the Lawn one hundred yards on either side. These accommodations are shaded behind brick arcades. Each of the ranges also features three brick buildings—Hotels A through F—dining halls for the ravenous young scholars.

Jefferson adopted Latrobe's suggestions because they conformed with his notion of basing the University on the Greek model. In his plan the professors lived in the Pavilions, upstairs, and lectured on the ground floors. Their charges, of course, lived alongside in the Lawn rooms. Thus, in homage to the Greeks, teachers and students were gathered together physically as well as intellectually. Among universities of the period, the "hobby" of Jefferson's old age was both beautiful in appearance and unique in concept.

Jefferson devoted all the energies of his last years to the University of Virginia. He was particularly interested in his large, domed Rotunda.

Construction of the "sphere within a cylinder" was begun in October of 1822. Using one of Andrea Palladio's sketchbooks, he based the structure on the Pantheon in Rome. The two lower levels contained oval classrooms and meeting halls. The uppermost level—the dome room—was designed as the school's library.

It was in the dome room of the Rotunda—still unfinished in November of 1824—that Lafayette was feted by Jefferson, Madison, and the citizens of Albemarle. The very first such public affair at the University of Virginia was indeed memorable. Four hundred guests were seated at tables arranged in three concentric circles. "The meats were excellent," recorded the *Virginia Herald*, "and each eye around us

beamed contentment." The first, of many, eloquent toasts to Lafayette resulted in a burst of cheering that echoed across the circular room.

Jefferson, unable to speak loudly due to an inflammation of the throat, handed a brief speech to another to read. "I joy, my friends, in your joy, inspired by the visit of this our ancient and distinguished leader," he had written. "His deeds in the war of independence you have heard and read . . . . He made our cause his own . . . In truth, I only held the nail, he drove it." The Marquis de Lafayette was so touched by his

old friend's tribute that he stood, grasped Jefferson's left hand, and wept out loud.

Completed in September of 1826, the Rotunda was the last of his beautiful buildings erected. Sadly, "the Sage of Monticello" had died on July 4, 1826—the fiftieth anniversary, to the day, of the adoption of the Declaration of Independence. He never saw the Rotunda as a finished work.

Ironically, a letter of Jefferson's appeared in the *National Intelligencer* the very day he died. "All eyes are opened, or opening to the rights of

Top: Morea, the home of natural philosophy professor Robert Emmet.

Middle: Edgar Allan Poe's room at the University-Number 13 "Rowdy Row."

Bottom: The Grounds photographed in the 1850s from the east.

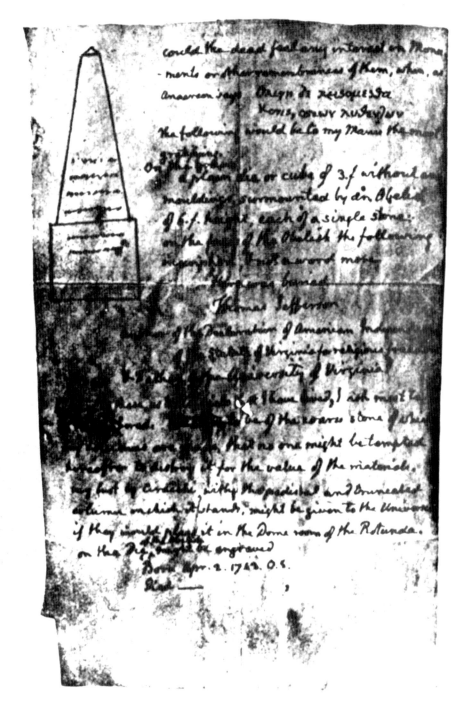

to well over 100. During the nineteenth century, some of the nation's most famous individuals were associated with Mr. Jefferson's "academical village." Edgar Allan Poe, for example, was a student for ten months in 1826. Interestingly, his room on the West Range was number thirteen. William Holmes McGuffey—the compiler of the best-selling McGuffey *Eclectic Readers*—held the chair of moral philosophy from 1845 until his death in 1873. John Singleton Mosby—later known as the "Gray Ghost of the Confederacy"—was expelled in 1852 after a shooting incident. Walter Reed, who helped conquer yellow fever, graduated from U.Va. Medical School in 1869. Future president Woodrow Wilson attended the law school in 1879 and 1880.

Throughout the 1800s University students diligently struggled to match the example set by the institution's illustrious, knowledge-hungry founder. "Enlighten the people generally," Jefferson had written, "and tyranny and oppressions of body and mind will vanish like spirits at the dawn of day."

Above: Jefferson's sketch for his obelisk-shaped tombstone.

Right: A typical University student of the late nineteenth century.

man," he had penned. "The general spread of the light of science has already laid open to every view the palpable truth, that the mass of mankind has not been born with saddles on their backs, nor a favored few booted and spurred ready to ride them legitimately, by the Grace of God." These were his last words to a grateful nation.

The University of Virginia—Jefferson's last, and greatest, gift to Albemarle County—opened its doors in March of 1825. The entering class that year numbered only forty students. Within twelve months, however, attendance had grown

CHAPTER VII

❖

*A Virginia slave auction, as pictured
by the* Illustrated London News.

*Despite playing a minor role in the advancement of mankind—as the birthplace of the authorof the Declaration—
Albemarle from its inception had been strapped with the practice of slavery. Lagging farm production also hampered
the county during this period even though internal improvements better connected Albemarle to the world.*

Slavery—the "Peculiar Institution"—had existed in Albemarle County since the first days of settlement. Bondsmen had been brought upriver into the Piedmont country to harvest its first money
crop, tobacco. In the early days an Albemarle planter calculated production, wrote John Hammond
Moore, "not in how many pounds of tobacco he could grow per acre, but by how many pounds were
produced annually per field hand."

It has been estimated that by the 1750s—during the days of "Big Albemarle"—around 2,000
slaves were laboring in the county's red-clay soil. They made up probably forty to forty-five percent
of the population. "Since many farmers owned only one or two blacks," penned Moore, "we can
assume most of them existed pretty much as members of the family, not unlike indentured servants,

Above: Enslaved African Americans in the field.

Bottom: Isaac Jefferson (1775-c.1850), a prominent member of Thomas Jefferson's enslaved community. At Monticello he labored as a blacksmith, tinsmith, and nailer.

working in the household or at their master's side in the fields. Few estates, if any, boasted more than fifty slaves, and rarely were these workers to be found in great numbers; instead, in groups of eight or ten they toiled away in isolated quarters...."

By the mid-1800s, however, the picture had changed—along with Albemarle's growing population, and the rise of an agrarian, or property-based, aristocracy. In 1820, for example, Albemarle counted within its borders 19,747 residents. Of that number 10,659 (or fifty-three percent) were enslaved African Americans. Ten years later the total population of the county was 22,618, of which 11,759 (or fifty-two percent) were slaves. Thirty years later—in 1860, on the eve of the bloody Civil War—enslaved blacks still comprised fifty-two percent of the county's population. Albemarle, in that year's census, boasted 26,625 inhabitants. Slaves numbered 13,916. Free blacks comprised less than three percent of the total population.

"Slaves were responsible for the majority of the labor on plantations in Albemarle County," wrote anthropologist Lynn Rainville in *The Magazine of Albemarle County History*. "They planted and harvested crops, cared for livestock, manufactured nails and craft goods, and built houses, mills, and railroads." Despite their importance to the local economy, however—and despite their large numbers—they labored in obscurity. Antebellum wills

and tax documents—such as those pertaining to Mt. Fair, the Brown family estate in western Albemarle studied by Rainville—today "evoke a very limited picture of a once-large, enslaved African American community." As examples, Rainville noted that one 1790 receipt states Bezaleel Brown was taxed "for owning three slaves. One of these individuals may have been 'Bettey,' a slave he inherited from his father...in 1762." A will from 1803 mentions "old negro woman Sarah." The documents hint at lives and relationships but offer very little that is substantial. Sadly, the people who had labored the most for Albemarle County shared not one whit in its profits, and where barely deemed worthy of notice.

Of course many believed them incapable of bettering themselves. Even "the Sage of Monticello" had been guilty of this bias. "Comparing them [the blacks] by their faculties of memory, reason, and imagination," he had written in his *Notes on the State of Virginia*, "it appears to me, that in memory they are equal to whites; in reason much inferior, as I think one could scarcely be found capable of tracing and comprehending the investigations of Euclid; and that in imagination they are dull, tasteless, and anomalous."

Unfortunately Jefferson, and others, convinced millions of this ugly proposition. Sir Augustus John Foster, however, had benefited from experience, and the ability to see that the

slaves' seeming lack of talent was due directly to the institution under which they had been subjugated. "That the black race is, however, as susceptible of refined civilization," he noted, "and as capable to the full of profiting by the advantages of education as any other of any shade whatever, must be admitted, in contradiction to Mr. Jefferson's prejudices, by any person who has had the honour to be acquainted with the daughters of Christophe, who was Supreme Sovereign of Haiti…and who spared no kind of expense in getting good European masters for his children."

In Albemarle the word "master" meant something quite different. "How [the slaves] fared day to day is pretty much a matter of conjecture," wrote Moore, "but we can assume, human nature being what it is, that their existence was tedious and humdrum…and subject to the caprice of the head of the family they served." Economic conditions notwithstanding, slavery was thriving in the shadows of the Blue Ridge Mountains.

With slavery came the particularly nasty business of trafficking in human beings. "Newspaper advertisements [of the antebellum era] seem to indicate," wrote researcher Gayle Schulman, "that several people in Albemarle County may have made their primary income as local slave traders." F. B. Dyer placed the following, for example, in the March 16, 1821 edition of the Charlottesville *Central Gazette*: "For Sale, A valuable woman and three boys; the woman about 25—the oldest of

the children about 6—she is one of the best serving women in Virginia, being a good Cook, Seamstress, Washer, Ironer, &c. and comes recommended with a character unexceptionable."

Two years later—on July 26, 1822—the same newspaper included this: "Negroes for Sale. Will be sold according to law, without reserve, in the town of Charlottesville…20 Likely Negroes." "Reading these documents," noted Schulman in the Magazine of Albemarle County History, "cannot fail to remind us that enslaved people were considered to be property—assets to be bought and sold or used as collateral to borrow money. This legal, social, and economic reality was assumed by generations before the documents reviewed here were recorded."

Fortunately, Albemarle could sometimes count among its residents, and neighbors, gentlemen who fought against those assumptions. Edward Coles was born at Enniscorthy, in the Green Mountain area of Albemarle County, on December 15, 1786. He was the seventh son of John Coles II, who had served as a patriot colonel in the Revolution. Enniscorthy was a 5,000-acre plantation tilled by bondsmen. Young Edward, therefore, grew up as a vested participant in the degrading enslavement of his fellow man.

Above: All that remains of Thomas Jefferson's Joinery, located along Mulberry Row atop Monticello Mountain.

Left: Number Nothing Court Square. Among the mottled black bricks— between the windows of the first and second stories—can still be read: "BENSON AND BRO. AUCTION ROOMS."

IMAGES COURTESY OF THE AUTHOR

Above: F. Edward Coles (1786-1868), a man who defied his family and defied the institution of slavery.

Right: Enniscorthy, the Coles family estate.

Born into the slavocracy, Coles became, on the recommendation of Jefferson, the private secretary of then-president James Madison. His perceptions, however, ran contrary to those prevailing amongst his peers. Upon receiving his inheritance—a plantation on the Rockfish River and twenty blacks, some of whom were probably his own half brothers and half sisters—he sold the property and in 1819 moved to Illinois, "carrying with him all his slaves, giving them their freedom," noted Woods in a rare mention, "and settling them by families on farms near Edwardsville." He freed them, Coles later wrote, "As a reward for their past services, [and] as a stimulant to their future exertions."

Albemarle aristocrat Edward Coles had struck a personal blow against the practice of slavery. His continued struggle against the "blighting curse" placed him among the leaders of the anti-slavery forces in Illinois. "He was appointed by [President James] Monroe first Governor of the Territory of Illinois," noted Woods, "and was elected its second Governor when it became a state...."

Gen. John Hartwell Cocke was another central Virginia anti-slavery man. "The distinguished and eccentric [gentleman] of Fluvanna," penned Woods, "though never a citizen of Albemarle, was yet much interested in its affairs through his connection with the University." He was one of its first Board of Visitors' members and, in order to guard the students from liquid temptation, an earnest promoter of the cause of Temperance. Cocke's most important contribution to central Virginia society, however, may have been his lifelong, outspoken opposition to slavery. He referred to it as "the great cause of all the great evils of our land." Slavery, he believed, was contrary to natural law and a mockery to the high ideals of the Declaration of Independence. Prophetically, the general warned that Virginians would be "overwhelmed, unless the cause [of slavery] is removed."

During the mid-1800s Albemarle's problems, noted Moore, "were merely those of the Old Dominion and much of the seaboard South in miniature. The very things that had created the region and bestowed considerable prosperity upon it in the eighteenth century became troublesome liabilities in the nineteenth." Slavery was becoming a burden, and "after 1820 the

system itself faced mounting criticism." Agriculture, he wrote, "had to contend not only with worn-out fields and problems presented by black servitude, it also faced mounting competition from new lands beyond the mountains." The new, western frontiers were not only challenging the Piedmont's status as an agrarian Eden, they were attracting the region's sons and daughters as well.

Nonetheless, Albemarle's towns were growing. By 1835, for example, twenty-seven post offices had been established in the county's growing settlements. Covesville during this period had thirty residents, as well as, according to Mary Rawlings, "one general store, one house of entertainment, one tan yard, one milliner . . . and one Presbyterian house of worship." Earlysville had a population of thirty-five, while Batesville, then-called Oliver's Old Store, counted twice that number. Also numbering seventy inhabitants was New York, situated in the western part of Albemarle between Brooksville and Afton. Milton—once the county's showcase river town—was already on its slow decline into nothingness. In 1835 it still counted, however, sixty whites and ten free blacks.

Charlottesville in 1835 was already Albemarle's biggest town. It featured, wrote Rawlings, "about 200 handsome and comfortable dwellings, generally of brick, four houses of worship, three large and commodious hotels, one tavern, two bookstores, two druggists' stores, and about 200 Mercantile establishments." Under this last heading were included one printing office—which issued a weekly newspaper—four tailor shops, three tan yards, three saddleries, two cabinet shops, three wheelwrights, one chairmaker, one house and sign painting business, and two coach and gig manufactures.

Legend
* Existing Buildings

1 Two houses built by Mrs Tracy Zigler
2 Noris' Blacksmith Shop
3 David Fowler - Cabinet Maker
4 John Thompkins - Carriage Maker
5 Origin unknown - Later General Store
6 Neal Residence
7 Mr Schroff - Tinner
8 Store built in 1781
9 John Benson - Residence & Business
10 Charles Day - Tailor
11 Nancy West - Residence & Business
12 John R Jones - Mercantile
13 James Leitch - 1770
14 Lyman Peck - Deputy Sheriff
15 Mercantile Store
16 Mrs Grant - Dry Goods Store
17 Jesse Scott - Fiddler
18 Old Barrack's owned by David Issacs
19 Issac Raphael - Residence & Business
20 Store & House owned by Nancy West
21 Joshua Grady - Blacksmith
22 Wm Summerson - Carpenter Shop
23 David Wolf - Grocery Store
24 Mathew Carey - House & Tenement
25 Mr Thomas' Residence
26 Market House
27 Presbyterian Church built 1828
28 Daniel Keith - Constable

29 Peter Lott Residence - before 1815
30 James Monroe - 1790 - later "Old Stone Tavern"
31 Store - Fleming & Boyd
32 David Fowler Res - built by Joel Pewell before 1773
33 John Yeargain - 1811 - Fine Liquors
34 Lewis Leschot - Swiss Jeweler
35 Public Library - founded by Harper & Southall
36 Storehouse by James Leitch
57 No 0° Mercantile with Slave Auction Block
58 Eagle Tavern - circa 1791
39 Post Office and Stores
40 Court House and Stone Jail
41 Mercantile Stores by John Kelly
42 John Cochran Residence
43 McKee's Row - (left to right)
    Thomas Wayt - Shop & Residence
    Andrew McKee - Shop & Residence
    Thos Wells & Geo Toole Res & Shop
    Bramham & Bibb - Dry Goods, Grocery
    Jno Simpson - Residence & Store
    Samuel Leitch - Residence & Store
    Printing Shop

44 Opie Noris Residence - 1814
45 V W Southall Residence - post 1829
46 Col John L Jones Residence - 1814
47 Christ Episcopal Church - 1824-26
48 Cornelius Schenk Residence - 1792
49 Hardin Davis - Postmaster
50 J A & Davis Residence - 1826
51 Valentine W Southall Residence
52 Dr Thos Jameson Residence - 1806
53 Swan Tavern - 1773 owned by John Jouett
54 Mrs Milly Jones Residence
55 The Rev Francis Bowman Residence
56 William Watson - Jailor
57 John Kelly Residence
58 Dr Raglands Widow

A View of Charlottesville, Virginia
circa 1828
Information based on "Early Charlottesville Recollections
of James Alexander, edited by Mary Rawlings and
Woods History of Albemarle County"

Left: Notice Court Square in the
upper right and Main Street running
along the lower left.

Below: Belmont, built c.1837, lent
its name to Charlottesville's
southeastern neighborhood.
IMAGE COURTESY OF THE AUTHOR

With a total population of 957—including 348 slaves and fifty-nine free blacks—the seat of Albemarle's government was making use of the services of fifteen professionals: three dentists, six physicians, and a like number of attorneys. Charlottesville also boasted a circulating library, a fire company, and its own thriving port—named Piraeus, after the port of Athens.

Scottsville, during this same period, came in at number two with about 600 inhabitants. The thriving James River port featured, according to Rawlings, "120 houses, chiefly of brick, two houses of worship, a male and female school, fourteen stores, one apothecary's shop . . . . a savings institution, two resident attorneys, [and] four regular physicians." Industrious Scottsvillians were manufacturing clothing, leather shoes, and earthenware. Albemarle's third largest gathering of souls in 1835 was the University of Virginia where 200 Southern scions were, in their better moments, studiously absorbed in their weighty texts.

Much of Albemarle's growth was aided by impressive internal improvements. A turnpike from Scottsville to Staunton, completed in

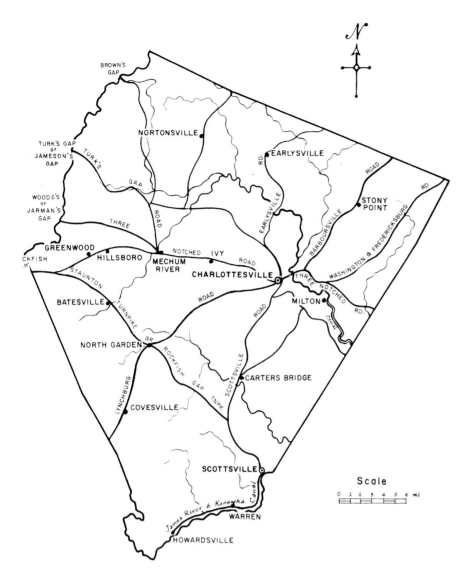

Railroads came to Albemarle in the decade before the Civil War. The Louisa Railroad—afterwards the Virginia Central and later the Chesapeake and Ohio—was extended to Charlottesville from the east in 1850. The first train chugged into the sleepy university town on June 27 of that year. "The line was continued westward," wrote Woods, "and reached Staunton in 1854." Tracks running between Charlottesville and Lynchburg, a segment of the Orange and Alexandria, were completed in 1860.

The region's most famous improvement, however, was the creation of Claudius Crozet. Born in France in 1789, Crozet had been educated at the renown Ecole Polytechnique (the institution after which West Point was modeled). As a second lieutenant of pontonniers he participated in the battle of Wagram and Napoleon's disastrous, 1812 invasion of Russia.

In 1849 Claude Crozet, by then Virginia's principal engineer, was called upon to supervise the drilling of a railroad tunnel through the Blue Ridge Mountains at Rockfish Gap. Over the next seven years the immense effort consumed a pile of money, uncounted man-hours, and dozens of lives. To reach Rockfish—to negotiate western Albemarle's rolling hills—Crozet first constructed a series of tunnels: one just west of

❖

Above: Albemarle County at the dawn of the railroad age.

MAP BY JOHN MIDDLETON FREEMAN.

Right: Claudius Crozet (1789-1864), the French engineer who pierced Afton Mountain.

1827, further encouraged commerce with the Shenandoah Valley. It quickly became as important as Albemarle's two other main thoroughfares: the Three Notched Road—"leading from Richmond to the Valley," wrote Moore, "and forming the main street of the village of Charlottesville"—and a north-south road running from Alexandria to Lynchburg which intersected with Three Notched "in the vicinity of Charlottesville." Benjamin Franklin Ficklin built, "at his own expense," wrote Rawlings, "a macadam road from Charlottesville to Scottsville and operated a stage between the two places; Scottsville then being the place where a majority of the students arrived by boat for the University." The river town gained further importance when the James River-Kanawha Canal—one of Virginia's great trade arteries—was completed in 1837.

Greenwood Station, 536 feet long; another at Brooksville spanning 864 feet; and a third, only 100 feet long, called "Little Rock." By comparison the main tube under the gap itself—called "the Blue Ridge Tunnel"—when completed stretched 4,264 feet.

On April 13, 1858, the first Virginia Central train pierced the hole at Rockfish. Although taking five years longer than anticipated, the French engineer—despite cost overruns and constant abuse by the press—had produced a public work of enduring utility. (Perhaps Crozet's greatest tribute is that his Blue Ridge Tunnel remained in use until 1944.)

These internal improvements, however, had not improved or indeed altered the horrible institution under which fully half of Albemarle's citizens labored. As the 1850s wound down the inevitable confrontation could no longer be forestalled.

The 1860 election was the last catalyst towards the nation's bloody subdivision. That year the population of the county was approximately 27,000. That number—closely mirroring Virginia statistics—was evenly divided between whites and enslaved African Americans. Six hundred free blacks also called Albemarle home. Charlottesville residents—counted in Albemarle's total—numbered 3,000, while 600 students were enrolled at the University.

When the Albemarle County votes were tallied in the November election John Bell (the Constitutional Union candidate) had received

1,317, carrying every precinct, with John C. Breckinridge (representing the Southern branch of the Democratic party) taking in 1,056. Not one single vote had been cast for Abraham Lincoln. Shortly thereafter, enthusiasm for the idea of secession—and armed conflict—began to build in Albemarle.

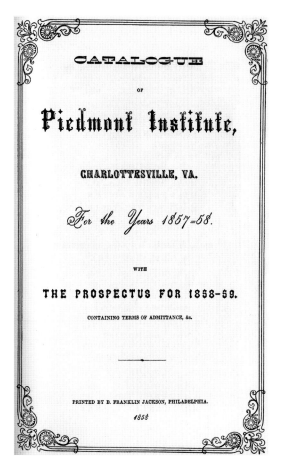

❖

Above: An 1860 five dollar bill featuring images of Jefferson and Monticello's garden entrance.

Left: Founded in 1853, the Piedmont Female Institute offered instruction in Latin, French, German, Spanish, Italian, painting, and music.

Chapter VIII

Albemarle in the Civil War

Albemarle supported the Confederate war effort by nursing wounded, producing food and materiel, and filling the rosters of over twenty companies with its own sons, husbands, and sweethearts. A raid led by General George Armstrong Custer was turned on its heels in 1864 but the flamboyant cavalryman returned one year later.

Confusion at Rio Hill—slashing Federal horsemen and the explosion of a Southern caisson.

The massive, pre-assault cannonade lasted close to an hour. As the shells whizzed overhead the men of the 19th Virginia Infantry—most of them sons of Albemarle—lay prone on the reverse slope of Seminary Ridge, immediately behind the Southern guns. They were there as part of Gen. Richard B. Garnett's Brigade, Pickett's Division, smack dab in the center of the infantry waiting to go forward. When the bombardment subsided, the 19th Virginia prepared to advance. They passed through the gun-line, dressed center on their newly issued battle flags, and fixed bayonets. A copse of trees and a low stone fence on the opposite ridge marked their goal. The date was July 3, 1863—Pickett's men were about to achieve immortality.

During the Civil War Albemarle County supported the Southern effort with all of its blood and treasure. Events had moved quickly after Abraham Lincoln's election. As early as December 5—two weeks before South Carolina's secession on the twentieth—U.Va. students sought, and received, permission from the faculty to raise volunteer units. The ranks of two student companies were quickly filled. Each numbering about seventy youngsters, the Sons of Liberty (dressed in red hunting shirts and black, doeskin trousers) and the Southern Guard (outfitted in blue shirts and baggy pantaloons) were soon drilling on the Lawn with antiquated flintlock muskets.

Four months later University students participated in a raid. On April 15, 1861, President Lincoln issued a call for 75,000 militia—which

included Virginia's quota of 2,340—to suppress the states already in rebellion. It was this request that tipped the scales in the Old Dominion. A state convention in Richmond adopted an ordinance of secession two days later. This vote was kept secret for nearly forty-eight hours so that the United States armory and arsenal at Harper's Ferry could be captured.

Taking part in this raid—which had been organized while Virginia was still in the Union—were the two U.Va. student companies, along with two Charlottesville volunteer militia units, the Monticello Guard and the Albemarle Rifles: together forming an ad hoc unit called the Charlottesville and University Battalion. Setting out from Charlottesville by train on the night of April 17, this force, along with other Virginia companies, reached Harper's Ferry late the next day. Although the federal detachment had destroyed considerable materiel before fleeing into Maryland, the mission was generally considered a success.

The war began in earnest on July 21, 1861, when the first major battle was fought northwest of Manassas, Virginia along the steep banks of Bull Run. The following day, in a driving rainstorm, 1,200 sick and wounded soldiers from the armies that had collided there arrived at the Charlottesville train station. "There was no one there to receive them," noted a letter in a Richmond newspaper, "and it was left to a few gentlemen and a handful of servants to transfer the sufferers, covered with dust and begrimed with

blood…to the distant buildings of the University. Soon all the public houses and the large halls rented for the purpose were overflowing…. Every day saw the same sorrowful sight repeated."

This was the commencement of what was soon designated the Charlottesville General Hospital. So quickly did this come about that just one month later a Richmond publication stated that "Charlottesville is now a vast hospital for the sick and wounded of our army." At first filling the public buildings at U.Va.—the Rotunda and its annex, the vacant student rooms—the hospital eventually also encompassed the Delavan on West Main, Midway on Ridge Street, the Monticello House downtown, and literally dozens of private homes.

During the course of the war the Charlottesville General Hospital, under the supervision of University professor James Cabell, admitted over 22,500 patients. Only 5,391 of these soldiers (or twenty-three percent) were suffering from gunshot wounds. Of these, 270 died here. The vast majority were afflicted with diseases like diarrhea, dysentery, malaria, pneumonia, tuberculosis (which was then called consumption), and typhoid. Of these something around 1,100 perished.

Relatively little is known about another local contribution to the Confederacy—the production of war materiel. Although Albemarle has never been considered a manufacturing region a surprising number of businesses churned out items needed by the Confederate Army.

Top: James Lawrence Cabell (1813-1889), University professor, Confederate surgeon, and head of the Charlottesville General Hospital.

Below: A row of headstones in Charlottesville's Maplewood Cemetery. Here rest a number of sick and wounded Southerners who arrived by train from Manassas.
IMAGE COURTESY OF THE AUTHOR

McKennie & Company, for example, opened in July of 1861 at Piraeus, the port of Charlottesville one mile east of town. There the enterprise's four employees, during the first year of operation, averaged eight to ten swords per week. Col. Marcellus McKennie, the owner, was the commander of the 88th Regiment of Virginia militia and a surgeon at the general hospital. In Howardsville T. D. Driscoll produced twenty-eight swords and sabers per week. Other military items produced in the county included infantry accoutrements—belts, cap boxes, cartridge boxes, shoes, and boots—as well as gun carriages, and harnesses for the artillery. The largest local concern producing war materiel was the Charlottesville Manufacturing Company—the business which afterwards became the Charlottesville Woolen Mills. During the conflict it produced cloth and uniforms for the Confederate Army.

During the war University of Virginia men served in every branch of the Southern military. At the outbreak there were scattered across the nation over 9,000 University alumni. Of this total some 2,500 served the Confederacy. Thirteen hundred became officers. About 500 U.Va. men lost their lives in the conflict. Of the twenty-six U.Va. alumni who became generals, perhaps the most famous were Lafayette McLaws, John Bankhead Magruder (who won the first little action of the war at Big Bethel,

Virginia, on June 10, 1861), and Philip St. George Cocke (who, because he commanded the military district along the Potomac, became known as "the first defender of Virginia"). Cocke was the son of Gen. John Hartwell Cocke and the only general officer, Northern or Southern, to commit suicide during the war.

Of the professors, Lewis Minor Coleman—who taught Latin—was mortally wounded at Fredericksburg. Basil L. Gildersleeve served on the staff of Gen. John B. Gordon. Albert Taylor Bledsoe became an assistant secretary of war. Without a doubt, however, the highest-ranking U.Va. Confederate was George Wythe Randolph, Thomas Jefferson's youngest grandchild. From March 22, 1862, until the following November he served as Jefferson Davis's secretary of war.

Albemarle County men served in the Confederate forces throughout the struggle. With the first flush of secession fever they volunteered into all three branches of the army. By the summer of 1861, in fact, close to 1,600 county men were in the Southern ranks. By the end of the war Albemarle and University men filled over twenty companies of artillery, cavalry, and infantry. "As in the 1770s," wrote John Hammond Moore, "county residents appear to have been generally united in a cause they thought right."

In the artillery branch, Albemarle boys worked the guns of the 1st and 2nd Rockbridge Artillery, the Albemarle Everett Artillery, and the Charlottesville Artillery organized by Capt. James McDowell Carrington. As horsemen they rode stirrup to stirrup in the Albemarle Light Horse (Co. K of the 2nd Virginia Cavalry) and the Albemarle Rangers (Co. F, 10th Virginia Cavalry).

Naturally, the vast majority of county boys shouldered muskets in the infantry. Aside from the local companies of provost guards—and militia units that were called out on occasion—Albemarle and U.Va. infantrymen fought in the 7th, the 56th, the 57th, and the 46th Virginia Regiments. In the last named, in fact, they filled the ranks of four companies. Albemarle native, Col. R. T. W. Duke, commanded the regiment.

The most famous unit in which local boys served, however, was the 19th Regiment Virginia Volunteer Infantry. During the war the 19th Virginia fought in ten battles and countless skirmishes. In the course of the war over 1,500

men served in the regiment. Its losses in combat—killed, wounded, captured, and missing in action—were well over 500. Another 300 suffered from the various diseases that ravaged the armies on both sides. Throughout, these citizen soldiers acquitted themselves well. As part of Gen. George E. Pickett's Brigade—and later under brigadiers Richard B. Garnett and Eppa Hunton—the 19th Virginia became known for its dependability, and steadiness under fire.

❖

Left: Dedicated in 1893, this monument alongside the University Cemetery marks the final resting place of 1,097 Confederate soldiers.

Below: The gravesite of Margaret Rion, the matron of the Midway Hospital.
IMAGE COURTESY OF THE AUTHOR

The 19th Virginia's first commander was 52-year-old West Point graduate Philip St. George Cocke. When Cocke was given a brigade he relinquished command to John Bowie Strange, a graduate of the first class at the Virginia Military Institute. Strange would remain in charge for sixteen months.

At First Manassas the 19th was held in reserve until the last minute. When they were moved forward into the fight they arrived just in time to see the Federal Army fleeing the field. The regiment first "saw the elephant," as the men used to say, at the Battle of Williamsburg on May 5, 1862. In that action it captured 200 Federals, and seven pieces of artillery. The 19th Virginia fought at Seven Pines—on June 1, 1862—suffering twenty percent casualties. At Gaines's Mill—on June 27—the regiment, with about 450 present for duty, played a major role in the final assault that broke the Union line. At Second Manassas, the 19th Virginia lost nearly 100 men assaulting Henry House Hill.

Then came Robert E. Lee's first invasion of the North. At Turner's Gap on Sunday, September 14, the regiment—numbering only 150—suffered sixty-three killed and wounded. Colonel Strange was mortally wounded. At the Battle of Sharpsburg three days later the unit counted only fifty-four officers and men. Fighting late in the action on the Confederate right the regiment lost eight killed and thirty-seven wounded (a staggering eighty-three percent).

Formed in May of 1861—at Manassas, Virginia—one of its ten companies came from Nelson County while Amherst County supplied two. Five companies hailed from Albemarle. They included Co. C, the Scottsville Guard; Co. D, the Howardsville Grays; Co. E, the Piedmont Guards; Co. F, the Montgomery Guard; and Co. K, the Blue Ridge Rifles. Companies A and B—the Monticello Guard and Albemarle Rifles respectively—came from the city of Charlottesville.

Back in Virginia the regiment rested and refitted in the Shenandoah Valley. Henry Gantt was appointed to command. At the Battle of Fredericksburg the regiment—as part of Pickett's Division—was posted in the center of the line and saw little action. In mid-February of 1863 Pickett's force was dispatched to Petersburg. The following month the brigade that included the 19th Virginia, under Gen. Richard B. Garnett, was detached for duty on the North Carolina coast.

They were recalled from the Old North State on April 29 to participate in Lee's second invasion of the North. If there was one experience that defined the Civil War for the men of the 19th Virginia Infantry, it was their participation in Pickett's Charge (fought during the Battle of Gettysburg's third day, July 3, 1863).

When Pickett's Division stepped off a hush fell over the combatants. Time froze. Somehow everyone on the battlefield realized it was a pivotal moment. The 19th Virginia—numbering that day 426—first came under fire as it neared the Emmitsburg Pike. Shells burst overhead, spraying the regiment with deadly shards of iron. Solid shot plowed into the ranks.

Scrambling over the fences lining the roadway they found themselves about 250 yards

Left: Gen. Robert E. Lee statue at Lee Park in downtown Charlottesville.
IMAGE COURTESY OF THE AUTHOR.

Below: The frock coat worn by the colonel of the 46th Virginia Infantry: R. T. W. Duke of Charlottesville.
IMAGE COURTESY OF LEWIS SAUNDERS

from the main enemy line. On the ridge the Federal gunners called for canister. Now the regiment entered the defending artillery's most deadly killing zone. With only twenty yards to go, the enemy fire became almost unbearable.

The men of the 19th Virginia Infantry, their thin ranks shrouded by thick smoke, leaned forward as if to steady themselves against a stiff gale.

Lunging forward the regiment gained the coveted stone fence. Here the fighting was hand-to-hand. Bayonets and sabers were used freely. Musket butts swung through the air accompanied by loud demands for surrender. A few Northerners did surrender, the balance retired but a short distance into the copse of trees. As the Federals drew away the 19th boys knelt behind the low wall and volleyed into them. They had gained their foe's defensive position but real victory required that they continue further. The enemy's center must be pierced.

But the attack was spent. From their tenuous position at the wall the men of the 19th Virginia could see an overwhelming enemy counterattack brewing. The regiment began to melt away. As the survivors stumbled back to Seminary Ridge they were reformed. It was feared that the enemy would launch a counter thrust. General Pickett passed among the men as they regrouped. To Lieut. "Nat" Wood the division commander extended his hand while almost sobbing out the words, "My brave men! My brave men!"

The one-hour action had cost the 19th Virginia 168 killed, wounded, and captured, a loss of thirty-nine percent. The regiment was

shattered—Pickett's Division was shattered. Although almost two years of war remained for the men of the 19th everything after Gettysburg was anti-climactic. The unit spent most of the following year at Chaffin's Farm on the James River below Richmond.

On June 3, 1864 the 19th Virginia Infantry assisted in the bloody repulse of the Federal assault at Cold Harbor. From mid-June until March of 1865 the regiment served in the trenches of the Howlett Line near Petersburg. The 19th Virginia Infantry participated in the fight at Hatcher's Run—on March 31—but fortunately escaped what Wood called "the defeat of the war" suffered by Pickett's Division at Five Forks on April 1. This, of course, was the beginning of the end.

Five days later—on April 6—the regiment, numbering no more than sixty officers and men, was surrounded on a hillside near Sailor's Creek in Amelia County. Half of the men surrendered. On Palm Sunday, April 9, twenty-nine survivors of the 19th Virginia Infantry furled their colors and stacked arms for the last time at Appomattox Court House.

During the war Albemarle County suffered two enemy incursions. The first took place on February 29, 1864. That day, 1,500 federal cavalrymen, under the command of Gen. George Armstrong Custer, thundered into Albemarle from the north and collided with a Confederate encampment. Dubbed the "Battle of Rio Hill," in reality it was nothing more than a skirmish.

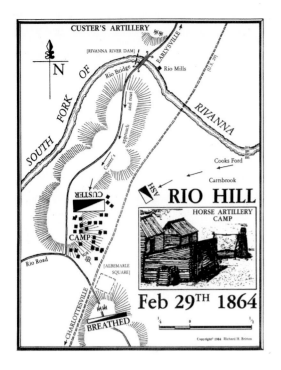

Top, left: The action of February 29, 1864, illustrated by the author.
IMAGE COURTESY OF THE AUTHOR

Top, right: General Philip "Little Phil" Sheridan.

Below: Depicting Custer's raid against Albemarle, these beautifully executed pages appeared as a center spread in Harper's Weekly.

The Federal high command had planned the raid against Albemarle to draw attention away from a larger attempt aimed at Richmond. Custer drew the assignment. He was ordered to capture Charlottesville and destroy the nearby railroad bridge over the Rivanna River. Any Confederate stores, munitions, and public buildings along the way would also be fair game.

Leaving Madison County in the pre-dawn hours, the Federal horsemen trotted into Albemarle County across its northern boundary. They continued unchallenged right on toward Rio Bridge (at the site of today's Rivanna dam). Charlottesville seemed ripe for plucking. Sitting astride Custer's route of march, however—one mile south of the span—was the winter camp of Confederate Gen. J. E. B. Stuart's Horse Artillery Battalion. Consisting of four batteries of light artillery—with sixteen field pieces and roughly 175 men—the battalion was under the temporary command of twenty-eight-year-old Capt. Marcellus Moorman. That winter they were camping in Albemarle in order to procure better grazing for the unit's 250 horses.

Right: Christopher Fowler, the Charlottesville mayor who surrendered the town to Sheridan and Custer on March 3, 1865.

Below: As a reward for thwarting Custer, the "Ladies of Charlottesville" presented this banner to "Stuart's Horse Artillery."

The entire affair lasted perhaps two hours. Reaching the Rivanna at 1 p.m., Custer dispatched a mounted column across Rio Bridge to attack the Southern camp. Meanwhile, Moorman's artillerymen, at last aware of the enemy's rapid approach, frantically rushed to hitch up their cannon and haul them to safety. A

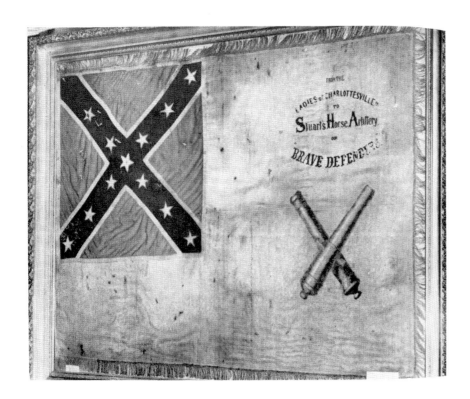

ridge to the south provided a convenient defensive line. There the rescued pieces were unlimbered into battery and immediately began lobbing shells back into their own camp, now awash in blue-jacketed horsemen.

There, too, Moorman had a stroke of genius. "The guns…were served with as few men as possible," wrote gunner George Neese, while several officers "formed the remainder of the artillerymen into a newly composed regiment of cavalry." An old Confederate battle flag waved from the line of gunners mounted on draft horses. Because of the paucity of sabers and small-arms, many of these Southerners were armed only with sticks and clubs.

Then lady luck intervened. With Northern cavalrymen slashing through the Confederate cabins one of the left-behind limbers exploded, showering the camp with shell fragments and wood splinters. Seeing the resulting confusion Moorman's mock Southern cavalrymen charged and drove Custer's men back over the Rivanna. In their retreat the Federals set fire to Rio Bridge and Rio Mills, a small community on the north bank. Charlottesville was spared for one more year.

On March 3, 1865, a 10,000-man Union cavalry army under the command of Gen. Philip Sheridan—the advance guard, ironically, under Custer—rode into Charlottesville virtually unopposed. That night the citizens of Charlottesville found themselves in the midst of a huge armed camp. Wasting no time Sheridan's horsemen appropriated bushels of corn and wheat and soon the Rivanna railroad bridge was laying in the waters it once spanned. Small raiding parties were dispatched while two Federal brigades destroyed the tracks between Charlottesville and Lynchburg. Sadly, several local households were ransacked.

The morning of Monday, March 6, the Charlottesville community sighed in relief as Sheridan's Army of the Shenandoah set out toward Lynchburg with bands blaring. They took with them hundreds of Albemarle County horses, wagon loads of confiscated foodstuffs, and close to 2,000 slaves.

Only a little over a month later, the haggard Albemarle veterans from Robert E. Lee's Army of Northern Virginia returned home after surrendering at Appomattox. For Charlottesville and Albemarle, the Civil War was over.

CHAPTER IX

ALBEMARLE IN THE LATE 1800s:

A NEW BEGINNING

*The end of the Civil War brought emancipation and military occupation. Black Baptist churches were
established and several African Americans rose to prominence. Industry, technology, and more railroads
modernized the county. In the century's final years Charlottesville became a city, Mr. Jefferson's Rotunda burned,
and one of Albemarle's own was named the nation's "most beautiful blonde."*

The war's end left Albemarle's white residents in a political, economic, and social abyss. Stunned
and disillusioned by the conflict's rapid denouement—especially in Virginia—they refocused on
farming, the county's original source of wealth. "Yet they found themselves in a strange, strange
world," penned John Hammond Moore, "an existence without slavery, filled with innumerable social
dislocations, and fraught with unanswered questions...."

Five days after Robert E. Lee's surrender President Abraham Lincoln was assassinated. Charlottesville
newspaperman James Alexander reportedly reacted to the news by joyfully repeating John Wilkes Booth's
defiant expletive, "Sic Semper Tyrannis!" Both of Alexander's sons had perished in the struggle. Other
Virginians, however, foresaw in the tragic event the coming consequences. "The South has lost her best

*Main Street Charlottesville—
lots of businesses and lots of mud.*

friend and protection," wrote ex-general George E. Pickett, "in this her direst hour of need."

On May 14 the 11th Pennsylvania Cavalry—600 troopers under the command of Lieut. Col. Franklin A. Stratton—trotted into downtown Charlottesville. Thus commenced Albemarle's military occupation. "[D]uring the next eight months," wrote William W. Reynolds in *The Magazine of Albemarle County History*, "this regiment, followed by two others, would provide the stabilizing force necessary for transition from a wartime environment to one of peace." Evidently Charlottesville was fairly trouble free—not so, western Albemarle. "Not many disorders have come to my notice," penned Stratton soon after his arrival, "but there is much need of a military post at this place...to protect the citizens from small bands of marauders and robbers investing various localities between here and the Blue Ridge."

Stratton's cavalrymen were eventually replaced by the foot soldiers of the 67th Ohio, followed by those of the 58th Pennsylvania. This last unit remained in Albemarle until January of 1866. "At that time," wrote Reynolds, "the districts and sub-districts in the state were discontinued, and in their place posts were established with small garrisons at selected points." Charlottesville became the headquarters for one company of the 11th U.S. Infantry. "For the most part these military rulers were fair and broadminded men," wrote Rev. Edgar Woods, "men who evidently tried to discharge their duties in the least odious and repulsive way." Occupying forces would remain in Albemarle until 1870 but at least the county's passage from chaos to order had been relatively calm.

Above: A prominent downtown enterprise.

Right: The steeple of Charlottesville's First Black Baptist Church, located on West Main Street.

IMAGE COURTESY OF THE AUTHOR

Other supposed "passages" were amazingly transitory. Historian Joseph C. Vance divided Albemarle's return to the Union into two periods: "Native Reconstruction" running from Lee's surrender until the spring of 1867, and "Congressional Reconstruction" from the last-named date until the Conservatives gained control in the July, 1869 elections. "In the first phase the Negro was more accurately a 'freeslave' than a 'freedman,'" wrote Vance. "This was true because, except for freedom of movement, the Negro operated in an economic and social framework which closely resembled the old slave system. That is, for practical purposes the old order was still operative, with control still in the hands of the old master class; a wage and share-cropping system simply had been substituted for ownership...."

Despite these circumstances some things were improving for the newly freed. With the conflict's end, several black Baptist churches rose up in Charlottesville and Albemarle County. To the first congregations, the very establishment of these churches was their first step toward independence. Their voices—lifted loudly in both prayer and song—were finally being heard.

In Charlottesville this movement had begun during the war at First Baptist Church on Park Street. As the conflict dragged on the congregation's black worshipers grew increasingly unhappy with their segregated status in the church. The Emancipation Proclamation—which took effect on January 1, 1863—spurred them to action. In March of that year the church's 800 enslaved members formally petitioned for the right to form their own separate organization. Fairfax Taylor—a former slave who had purchased his own freedom—was undoubtedly among the leaders of this effort.

The petition was granted and soon thereafter the new organization was worshipping in the parent church under the guidance of Rev. John T. Randolph, a white man. The list of later ministers includes Scottish-born Rev. James H. Fife, who built Oak Lawn and after whom Fifeville was named. The church's first black preacher was William Gibbons, an ex-slave possessed of "dynamic force and zeal." His wife, Belle Gibbons, was one of central Virginia's first public school teachers.

In 1867 the black Baptists began holding services on West Main Street in the basement of the Delavan Hotel (also called the "Mudwall" because of its dark-colored stucco). The congregation purchased the forty-year-old building the following year. After the dilapidated structure was torn down in 1876, the devoted congregants—most of them farm laborers—raised $7,000 and constructed a new church of brick. The First African Baptist Church of Charlottesville, at the corner of 7th and West Main streets, was dedicated on January 2, 1884.

Mount Zion Baptist Church at 105 Ridge Street—the second black Baptist church in Charlottesville—was formed in 1867. That same year Union Run Baptist church was built in Albemarle County on land deeded to the black congregation by Thomas Jefferson Randolph, the "sage of Monticello's" favorite grandson. The first pastor was Robert Hughes whose father, Wormley Hughes, had been the ex-president's principal gardener.

The two years of Virginia's "Congressional Reconstruction—from 1867 to 1869—were ones of great turmoil, even for Albemarle. "In essence," wrote Moore, "Radical Republicans, in firm control of Congress...reaffirmed military rule throughout the South and insisted the 'freeslave' must become a free man with all rights of citizenship secured by new state constitutions." Fairfax Taylor, the ex-slave, could not have agreed more. At Albemarle's first mixed-race political assembly—held at the Delavan in April of 1867—he demanded for blacks the right to serve on juries and attend the

Above: Fairfax Taylor (1816-1895), was buried in Maplewood Cemetery.
IMAGE COURTESY OF THE AUTHOR.

Below: Rural western Albemarle.

University of Virginia. Within months Taylor gained the support of the majority of Albemarle's freedmen—who outnumbered county whites by a solid margin of 2,500.

And Fairfax was not the only politically active Taylor. In September of 1867—when Albemarle choose its delegates to a much-anticipated constitutional convention to be held in Richmond—one of the nominees was James T. S. Taylor, Fairfax's son. Taylor the younger won the nomination, despite his father's announcement that he would not vote for his own progeny. The resulting "Underwood Convention," as it was called, sat until April of the next year with its main accomplishments being the incorporation into the new constitution of a provision for a new public school system and the "iron clad" test oath of allegiance—which, if retained, would disenfranchise ex-Confederates.

Tempers flared during the summer of 1868. A crowd of 150 armed blacks gathered near Clover Hill—and threatened the lives of several Conservatives—after discovering the body of an African American man they thought had been murdered. A riot was narrowly averted. The Charlottesville *Chronicle*, for its part, was not above attempting to unify white Conservatives by printing threats and racial diatribes. The editor hinted in one instance that for the more serious crimes perpetrated by freedmen, lynch law

should be administered. Fortunately, nothing of the sort happened. In his research, Vance found "no evidence of mob violence or 'K.K.K.' activity in Albemarle reconstruction."

In the end the U. S. Grant administration intervened—establishing "a popular referendum on the new constitution," noted Vance, "with separate voting on the objectionable clauses"—and a coalition between Conservatives and Moderate Republicans won the governor's race. "This resulted," wrote Vance, "in the acceptance of the constitution without the test oath…and the end of Radical control in Virginia." In January of 1870 Congress re-admitted the Old Dominion to the Union of states. "The political 'reconstruction' of Albemarle and Virginia," wrote Moore, "was over."

With political reconstruction out of the way physical reconstruction could begin in earnest. Central Virginia's railroads had been devastated—literally destroyed—by the war. There was much work to do, and eventually much Albemarle produce to be transported elsewhere.

In 1872, the Orange, Alexandria, and Manassas—which operated a line from Charlottesville to Lynchburg—laid additional tracks to Danville, and the Washington City, Virginia Midland, and Great Southern was born. Renamed the Virginia Midland following a reorganization, by 1885 it was operating fairly profitably. That year the rails carried through Charlottesville, among other items, livestock, cement, over 136,000 barrels of flour, and 3,500 barrels of whiskey. Passengers on the line paid a whopping 2.66 cents per mile. Though the rate was low so were the standards of passenger service. The cars were chilly, the seats were stiff, and the riding was often quite rough. The depots were no better. "They were often drafty buildings," wrote Vera Via, "too small to be comfortable." The Charlottesville Virginia Midland Railroad Station, in fact, was described as a "pig-sty."

Charlottesville's other railroad was the Chesapeake and Ohio Railway Company, the 1868 successor to the old Virginia Central. The C. & O. line ran west from Newport News, through Richmond and Charlottesville, to the Big Sandy River in West Virginia. The C. & O. literally put Charlottesville on the map. In 1870 alone, for example, over 47,000 passengers made use of its Charlottesville station. Because of this traffic both railroads constructed repair shops in the university town. At the downtown terminal the C. & O. also established a round-house and a machine shop.

Two railroads meant two separate depots. To make connections travelers were forced to either hire a hack or foot the mile-long stretch of pot-marked road. In 1885 Union Depot was erected where the rail lines crossed (between downtown and the University). The Charlottesville *Jeffersonian Republican* described the station as featuring "two reception rooms, baggage room, ticket office, restaurant, and a covered platform for protection from the sun and rain." The paper also proudly maintained that "Charlottesville has the handsomest depot in Virginia." Perhaps, but a reporter from the *New York Times* wrote that "the only sign of civilization [at the station] is a row of little stands loaded with fried chicken, home-made and home-sick cakes, 'cone' bread, buttermilk, and fruit."

Albemarle's most prominent manufacturing firm during this period was the Woolen Mills. Located one mile east of Charlottesville's original section—at the triangle of land between the Rivanna and Moore's Creek—it had been founded circa 1840 as the "Charlottesville Factory." John Adams Marchant purchased the enterprise in 1851. His son, Henry Clay Marchant—a disabled veteran of the 12th Virginia Infantry—took over the business in 1864, renamed it the

"Charlottesville Woolen Mills," and immediately began making improvements. "A factory building forty-five feet square with a basement and two upper floors was quickly constructed," wrote Harry E. Poindexter, "and as the new machinery arrived it was installed." Positive results were soon apparent. By 1872 annual sales had grown to $70,000.

Six years later the "Woolen Mills" began using Albemarle's first telephone system. When the manager "wishes to communicate with the mills he springs a signal button," wrote a local reporter, "and that strikes an electric bell at the mills…. Then [the manager] adjusts his instrument and every word over the line is heard distinctly by him."

One reason for the firm's success was its specialization. Echoing its Civil War output, the

Above: Henry Clay Marchant. Note the resemblance to Robert E. Lee.

Below: The Charlottesville Woolen Mills in the 1890s.

"Charlottesville Woolen Mills" in the 1880s began producing uniforms and military fabrics, albeit finer ones. It soon gained a national reputation for excellence. Municipal employees of Philadelphia, Chicago, and a number of other cities, for example, were at one time wearing Charlottesville-manufactured cloth. Eventually the mill was furnishing the clothing for, according to Poindexter, "ninety percent of the military schools in the United States, including West Point."

In 1882 the mill complex employed sixty hands. Ten years later the business, wrote William E. Webb, "paid in wages to its 115 employees, one-third of whom were women, the sum of $45,000." This prosperity, naturally, helped build up the neighborhood. In the nearby workers' village a beautiful wooden chapel was erected during the late 1880s.

While big things were happening along the Rivanna, little Charlottesville—one mile to the west atop a commanding ridge—was finally coming of age. "Incorporation of Charlottesville as a city," penned Moore, "clearly was a very important event on the local scene. In February 1888, close on the heels of a mass meeting urging such action, the General Assembly granted a municipal charter." That year the new city numbered 5,000 inhabitants. These urban folks were experiencing modernization and growth at an ever-quickening pace.

Street cars—the first drawn by horses or mules—had arrived in 1887. Electric ones soon followed. "A large number of land and development companies," wrote Susan Holbrook Perdue, "came about because of the transportation opportunities." These included, according to Perdue, "the Charlottesville Industrial and Land Improvement Company (1889), the Charlottesville West End Land Company (1890), and the Belmont Land Company (circa 1890)." The county seat was "abandoning its swaddling clothes," as Moore so aptly wrote, and "one can see outlines of the twentieth-century community which would evolve."

The view of the future was temporarily blotted out, however—on October 27, 1895—by a column of smoke rising from the University of Virginia. The Rotunda was ablaze. Erupting in the Annex—an ungainly attachment completed in 1852—the flames soon spread to Thomas Jefferson's beautiful homage to the Pantheon.

Students, faculty, and firefighters battled the fire for several hours but eventually they yielded to the inevitable. The centerpiece of Jefferson's "academical village"—his most palpable educational legacy—was gutted.

The conflagration "was so sudden, so unexpected, so startling in its occurrence; so destructive in its physical consequences; so far reaching in its moral influence," wrote Philip Alexander Bruce, "that it can, with perfect accuracy, be taken as a milestone to mark the close of one period and the opening of another." A tremendous shock to the Charlottesville community as well, Virginius Dabney called it "a catastrophe of the first magnitude."

The University administration responded to the crisis with unshaken determination. "The ruins were still smoldering," wrote Dabney, "when the faculty met that afternoon and resolved, despite the disaster, to carry on the work of the University." Classes were held the next day, albeit in rearranged and makeshift lecture halls. And, within a short time, New York architect Stanford White was selected to reconstruct the burnt-out ruin. Over the objections of a few he rebuilt the interior in the classical-Renaissance "Beaux Arts" style.

For nineteenth-century Charlottesville one last drama remained. Maud Coleman Woods

Right: Woods's headstone in Maplewood Cemetery. "Blessed are the pure of heart, for they shall see God."

IMAGE COURTESY OF THE AUTHOR.

Bottom: Maud Coleman Woods—of Ridge Street, Charlottesville—the nation's most beautiful blonde.

FROM MISS AMERICA BY ALEXANDER BLACK.

was the extremely attractive blue-eyed daughter of Micajah Woods—Albemarle's commonwealth's attorney—and his wife, Matilda Morris Minor Woods, of High Street. Born in 1877, she was compared in print to Hebe—the Greek goddess of youth, spring, and vigor—and referred to as "Virginia's loveliest daughter." She also possessed a modest charm perfectly befitting a young lady of the period.

An influential Charlottesvillian, in 1898 Micajah Woods was also a prominent member of the United Confederate Veterans. That same year lovely Maud, at a veterans' reunion, was chosen—and photographed—as one of the convention's "Rosebud Garden of Girls." Soon thereafter Alexander Black, a New York writer and photographer—having seen the aforementioned poses—took several shots of Maud at her Charlottesville home for a book entitled *Miss America*. Black promised that he would not identify the young lady by name—a special condition required by the mores of the time and demanded by the old Confederate, her father.

Then, in the summer of 1900, the Woods family received a tremendous shock via telegram. Twenty-three-year-old Maud had been chosen as America's "most beautiful blonde." The competition had been hosted by the *New York World* for the following year's Pan American Exposition to be held in Buffalo. Her image was to be reproduced on the exposition's official seal. Unbeknownst to the Woods family, Alexander Black had submitted Maud's photograph, and identified her to the world. Within days Maud's likeness—and name—appeared on the front pages of all the largest newspapers in the United States. Micajah Woods was beside himself in anger. "Oh, Papa," Maud reportedly exclaimed, "I am so mortified."

In order to escape the unsavory publicity, Maud retreated to Claremont, a family estate on the James River. There she contracted typhoid, and there she died on August 24, 1901—one day after her twenty-fourth birthday. Like a small candle that flickers too brightly, Maud Coleman Woods's radiance lit up the last year of the Victorian age—and was soon extinguished.

It was a fitting analogy, perhaps, to Albemarle's introduction to the modern world. The twentieth century had arrived, like it or not, and with it was coming a new set of morals, along with new technologies, new advancements, and new wars. Those regions rooted in history and tradition—like Albemarle County—could either die fighting for their past, or adapt. Thus was drawn to a close Albemarle and Charlottesville's first 150 years.

BIBLIOGRAPHY

Thomas Anburey, *Travels Through the Interior Parts of America In a Series of Letters* (London, 1789).

George W. Bagby, *The Old Virginia Gentleman and Other Sketches* (New York, 1910).

Jacques Pierre Brissot, *New Travels in the United States of America, 1788* (Cambridge, 1964).

Andrew Burnaby, *Travels Through the Middle Settlements in North America* (New York, 1970).

David I. Bushnell Jr., "The Five Monacan Towns in Virginia, 1607," Smithsonian Miscellaneous Collections (Washington, 1937).

John Edwards Caldwell, *A Tour Through Part of Virginia in the Summer of 1808* (Richmond, 1851).

Charlottesville 200th Anniversary Commission, "Charlottesville 1762—1962" (Charlottesville, 1962).

Maj. Gen. Marquis de Chastellux, *Travels in North-America in the Years 1780—81—82* (New York, 1827).

Cecile Wendover Clover and F. T. Heblich, Jr., *Holsinger's Charlottesville, A Collection of Photographs by Rufus W. Holsinger* (Charlottesville, 1995).

Noble E. Cunningham, Jr., *In Pursuit of Reason: The Life of Thomas Jefferson* (New York, 1987).

Virginius Dabney, *Mr. Jefferson's University, a History* (Charlottesville, 1981).

———————, *Virginia, The New Dominion: A History from 1607 to the Present* (New York, 1971).

John H. Gwathmey, *Twelve Virginia Counties: Where the Western Migration Began* (Richmond, 1937).

Thomas Jefferson, *Notes on the State of Virginia* (Chapel Hill, 1954).

K. Edward Lay, *The Architecture of Jefferson Country: Charlottesville and Albemarle County, Virginia* (Charlottesville, 2000).

Henry "Light Horse Harry" Lee, *The American Revolution in the South* (New York, 1969).

Ben C. McCary, *Indians in Seventeenth-Century Virginia* (Charlottesville, 1957).

John Hammond Moore, *Albemarle: Jefferson's County, 1727—1976* (Charlottesville, 1976).

Dumas Malone, *Jefferson the Virginian* (Boston, 1948).

Susan Holbrook Perdue, "'The Best of Country Life:' A Progressive Model Subdivision for a University Town in Charlottesville, Virginia, 1909–1917" (unpublished manuscript, 2005).

Mary Rawlings, *The Albemarle of Other Days* (Charlottesville, 1925).

William W. Reynolds, "Military Occupation of Albemarle County: May, 1865–January, 1866," *The Magazine of Albemarle County History* (Charlottesville, 1998), 56:39—52.

Eudora Ramsay Richardson, *Jefferson's Albemarle: A Guide to Albemarle County and the City of Charlottesville, Virginia* (Charlottesville, 1941).

Emily J. Salmon and Edward D. C. Campbell, Jr., Editors, *The Hornbook of Virginia History: A Ready-Reference Guide to the Old Dominion's People, Places, and Past* (Richmond, 1994).

Gayle M. Schulman, ""Site of Slave Block?" *The Magazine of Albemarle County History* (Charlottesville, 2000), 58:65—87.

Joseph C. Vance, "Race Relations in Albemarle During Reconstruction," *The Magazine of Albemarle County History* (Charlottesville, 1954), 13:28—45.

Dr. Alan Williams, "The Road to Independence: Virginia 1763—1783" (Richmond, 1976).

Rev. Edgar Woods, *History of Albemarle County in Virginia: Giving some account of what it was by nature, of what it was made by man, and of some of the men who made it* (Charlottesville, 1901).

SHARING THE HERITAGE

historic profiles of businesses,

organizations, and families that have

contributed to the development

and economic base of Albemarle & Charlottesville

W. E. Brown, Inc. 72
Core Knowledge Foundation 76
Thomas Jefferson Foundation 79
ACAC Fitness and Wellness Centers 80
Hampton Inn & Suites at the University 82
Rivanna Farm 84
NAEVA Geophysics, Inc. 86
Richard A. Oliva & Sons, Inc. 88
Albemarle County 90
City of Charlottesville 91
Chase Investment Counsel Corporation 92
Allied Concrete Company 94
Hospice of the Piedmont 96
Albemarle Charlottesville Historical Society 98
Boar's Head Inn 99
Carlisle Motion Control Industries, Inc. 100
Richmond & Fishburne, L.L.P. 101
Stevens & Company 102
Mincer's University of Virginia Imprinted Sportswear 103
Our Lady of Peace 104
Hantzmon Wiebel, L.L.P. 105
McLean Faulconer, Inc. 106
W.A. Lynch Roofing Company, Inc. 107
McGuireWoods L.L.P. 108
Residence Inn by Marriott 109
Martha Jefferson House 110
A. Scott Ward 111
Heritage Memorials, Inc. 112
Innisfree, Inc. 113
John Linkous Volkswagen, Inc. 114
Charlottesville Regional Chamber of Commerce 115
Bank of America 116
Carmello's 117
Blue Ridge Home Builders Association 118
Gold's Gym 119

SPECIAL THANKS TO

Residence Inn by Marriott

W. E. BROWN, INC.

W. E. Brown, Inc. has been installing and servicing plumbing, heating, ventilating, air conditioning and electrical services for the central Virginia area since 1922. During these eight decades, the company has evolved from a small "backyard" plumbing company into a full-service plumbing, mechanical and electrical contracting firm.

The firm was originally named Brown & Johnson. Founded by W. E. "Willie" Brown and Guy Johnson, it opened up in a little building on Second Street Southwest between what is now the Downtown Mall and Water Street. The company stayed in this location from 1922 to 1928, until Brown and Johnson decided to go their separate ways.

From 1928 to 1942, Brown and Preston Taylor, who had been a salesman calling on Brown & Johnson, joined forces and decided to open up in a larger building in the 500 block of West Main Street, across the street from the Ford Lincoln Mercury Dealership, which has now become the West Main Station Building.

Prior to this move the company provided plumbing and hot water heating and, with the move to West Main, they began to sell appliances, which was Taylor's expertise. While the company seemed to flourish during this time, the economy slid with the onslaught of the Depression, and the company faltered and had to close its West Main facility and split up the operation.

Brown had to go back to his garage shop in the backyard of his home on Douglas

Above: Historic renovation project for the Fluvanna County Courthouse in the early '70s shows an example of continuous baseboard forced air heating and cooling used to fully hide the modern system installation from view.

Below: Design builds project for UVA Darden School modernization and energy consumption reduction.

Avenue in Charlottesville's Belmont neighborhood where he operated the business from 1943 to 1950.

In 1945, M. P. "Duke" Martin, who had been dating Brown's daughter, Barbara, for quite some time, came back from military service and joined the family firm on a full-time basis. By that time Martin had begun to add additional services to the company, including forced air heating, which went along with the hot water heating. This required the addition of sheet metal services, and thus was born the Sheet Metal Division of W. E. Brown, Inc.

In 1950 the company bought four lots on Monticello Road from Mrs. Maupin, who lived in a home which fronted Belmont Avenue. Maupin had used these lots for her garden for years. The company built a small cinder block building of approximately twenty-four feet by eighty feet that is still part of the company's offices today.

The company continued to grow through the sheet metal services and quickly needed to expand to accommodate the work being done. The company doubled the width of the building in 1954, and added a wing on the rear, which became the sheet metal shop.

W. E. Brown began his career as a plumber's apprentice in 1916. His master plumber's license, issued by the City of Charlottesville in September 1924, is thought to be the oldest such license in the city.

The family-owned firm is now in its third generation. Brown's daughter, Barbara has worked in the family business since she was twelve years

old, and her husband, Merritt "Duke" Martin, entered the business after the war in 1944. Brown's son, Gene, was president of the firm from 1963 until 1978. Barbara and Merritt's son, John Martin, took the reins in 1978 and has been with the company full time since 1976.

"We've always been a family-owned company and that atmosphere is reflected throughout the firm, " says John Martin. "We have several second- and third-generation employees including fathers and sons and fathers and daughters." Several husbands and wives also work for the firm, including John Martin's wife, Amy.

The firm was incorporated in 1953 and continues to operate at 915 Monticello Road. The original building has doubled in size from the 1950s and a second floor on top of the building was built in 1988 as the company acquired the competing firm of Ray Fisher Inc., which was in the HVAC & electrical business.

As the company has continued to expand and grow, a ninety by twenty-four-foot, two-story shop and warehouse addition was constructed in 2003 on the west side of the property, when the company acquired the house next door. In addition to the expansion done over the last ten years, the company purchased the two houses on the east side of the shop, demolishing one for additional parking and remodeling one for rental use at the time.

W. E. Brown, Inc. has grown considerably in recent years and now employs almost one hundred people. The company's fleet of fifty plus vehicles serves Charlottesville and Albemarle County as well as the surrounding counties of Nelson, Louisa, Greene, Orange, Fluvanna, Buckingham, and portions of Culpepper.

W. E. Brown, Inc. started business as a residential plumbing and heating firm but later branched out into commercial construction.

Above: A new heating and cooling system being installed for The Enterprise Center on Market Street during the expansion and conversion to an office complex.

Below: An example of a water source heatpump system being installed to serve a custom home.

The firm's services expanded as heating, air conditioning, and ventilation products became more sophisticated. An electrical contracting division was added to the firm's list of services in the 1950s.

The importance W. E. Brown, Inc., placed on quality is illustrated by its almost unequivocal one-year guarantee. The guarantee reads: "If within a period of one year after original installation any part or portion of the products furnished and installed by W. E. Brown, Inc., shall prove to be defective in material or workmanship, the corporation will repair or exchange such part or portion.

"The guarantee covers plumbing, heating, air conditioning electrical wiring or any of the new installation services rendered by W. E. Brown, Inc.

"Further: We guarantee our heating systems to heat to seventy degrees in zero weather, our air conditioning to maintain specified temperatures of contract (seventy-two to seventy-eight degrees for residences with a ninety-five degree dry bulb outdoor temperature).

"This guarantee is limited to a period of one year from date of original installation, except for specific guarantees of products by manufacturers in excess of one year."

Although this demonstration of confidence in the quality of work performed was unusual in those days, it is very limited when compared with a water heater guarantee the company gave its customers in the late 1940s. At that time, Brown put a ten-year guarantee on a water heater that was backed up for only one year by the manufacturer. Even with this generous guarantee, the firm never had to replace a single heater.

The company files at W. E. Brown, Inc., are filled with thousands of testimonials from satisfied customers. Many are professionally prepared on company letterhead but most are simple, handwritten expressions of thanks from individual customers.

For example, the National Trust for Historic Preservation wrote to thank the company for work done at Montpelier, the home of President James Madison. "The job was completed efficiently and with the smallest possible inconvenience," the letter read. A handwritten note from a residential customer said, "I have nothing but praise for the courteous and efficient service rendered by your work crew. They were terrific!"

W. E. Brown, Inc., believes strongly in ongoing training programs for both new and longtime employees. The firm is heavily involved in the training programs offered through Charlottesville Albemarle Technical

Education College (CATEC) and two employees also teach at the school. These programs ensure that company employees are skilled in all the latest techniques and technologies of their particular trade.

W. E. Brown, Inc., is involved in new construction for both residential and commercial customers but also maintains a strong service department.

"Our customers know they can always depend on us when any of their systems need service," comments Martin.

Because of its reputation for quality and service, W. E. Brown, Inc., has been selected to help restore many of the historic buildings in Charlottesville and surrounding areas. These include Ash Lawn, the home of President James Monroe; Kenmore Plantation in Fredericksburg; Sully Plantation in Fairfax County; and the Levy Opera House in Charlottesville. The firm has also been called on to provide services at Monticello, home of President Thomas Jefferson.

The company archives still contain a yellowed proposal for plumbing work at Charlottesville's venerable Paramount Theater in 1932. Cost of the project, which included installation of hot and cold water lines into the boiler room, was $143, including labor and materials. The proposal, however, specifically excluded "moving any coal in the coal room" in order to complete the project.

In addition, W. E. Brown has provided heating, air conditioning and plumbing for more than forty area churches, a number of schools and many projects at the University of Virginia.

The company also does restoration work that's not on such a grand scale. Over the years company employees have recovered more than one set of false teeth for owners who let them slip...right into the commode.

Since it was founded eight decades ago, W. E. Brown, Inc., has been guided by a set of principles that are clearly expressed in the firm's mission statement:

"Our mission in the twenty-first century is simply Service Today. To be successful, we rely on the talents of our employees and their commitment to deliver a project that equals or exceeds the expectations of the customer and end user. This is achieved

through teamwork, diligence, creative ideas, mutual respect for all participants, on-going training and development, and continuous evaluation of our successes or failures at meeting these goals. To assure that we fulfill these commitments, we will attempt to provide the necessary financial resources for personal and corporate growth and expansion; and the utilization and integration of the latest technologies of our industry into the normal operations of our business.

"It is this commitment to our customers that gives us our history and guarantees our future."

Above: Fellini's Restaurant renovation and building preservation done by the owner to preserve one of Charlottesville's unique eateries.

Below: An example of a new geothermal pumping system being installed for a modern indoor heating and cooling system in a home that is over a hundred years old.

CORE KNOWLEDGE FOUNDATION

To call E. D. Hirsch, Jr., a reformer would be an understatement. As the author of such influential books as *Cultural Literacy* and *The Schools We Need and Why We Don't Have Them*, Hirsch promoted the idea that to function and prosper effectively in society, children must be exposed to an academically rich environment.

In 1986, Hirsch retired from a distinguished career in the English Department of the University of Virginia and established a foundation dedicated to reforming education by focusing on its most serious shortcomings. He felt the main shortcoming was a bland, unfocused curriculum that left children without the solid content knowledge necessary for advanced work, for active citizenship, for understanding their own culture, and for grasping how their culture fits into the larger world picture.

In short, Hirsch's goal is to restore the literal meaning of liberal education. To achieve this goal, he formed The Core Knowledge® Foundation, an independent, nonprofit, nonpartisan organization headquartered in Charlottesville. The Foundation conducts research on school curricula, develops books

Above: Fifth graders in Texas explore plant classification.

and other materials for parents and teachers, offers workshops for teachers, and serves as the hub of a growing network of Core Knowledge Schools.

"Core Knowledge has been a small but powerful influence on the American educational scene," says Dr. Barbara Garvin-Kester, president of the Core Knowledge Foundation. "The legacy I desire for this organization is to have it assume the starring role in transforming American education."

Core Knowledge is based on a belief that knowing how to think depends on having something to think about. Founder Hirsch explained this concept with four key points:

* More knowledge makes you smarter;
* Working to increase knowledge has a measurable effect;
* The more broad, general knowledge you acquire in childhood, the more broadly competent you become as an adult; and
* By giving everyone more knowledge, we can make everyone more competent, creating a more just society and a citizenry more capable of making intelligent choices.

The Core Knowledge Foundation helps schools to implement a specific, academically rich curriculum called the *Core Knowledge Sequence*. It does this by:

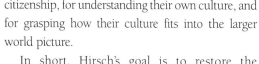

- Publishing books describing and supporting the curriculum, sometimes in partnership with other publishers, and publishing a newsletter, *Common Knowledge*, now in an electronic format.
- Maintaining a website to explain its philosophy and programs, to provide teacher resources, to empower teachers within its network to share lesson plans, to present its publications, to inform its clients about other educational resources, and, when possible, to share the evaluations and assessments of independent researchers.
- Providing professional development and implementation advice through staff members and a number of consultants with Core Knowledge experience who are based in various parts of the country.
- Holding an annual three-day conference preceded by three days of preschool institutes.
- Influencing policymakers, legislators, educators, parent groups, and teachers to embrace education reforms that provide a strong foundation of content-based knowledge.
- Offering college course outlines free on the foundation website and in CD form. Entitled *What Elementary Teachers Need to Know*, this series of outlines encourages schools of education to teach a more content-driven curriculum and to help teachers to prepare their students to meet the subject standards now in place in most states.

There are now more than 500 Core Knowledge schools in 46 states, as well as 350 preschools.

The Board of Directors of Core Knowledge includes a number of well-known and

Above: Virginia preschoolers build Core Knowledge language and movement coordination skills.

Below: Founder of Core Knowledge E. D. Hirsch, Jr.

influential individuals. As of January 2005, the Board included Dr. E. D. Hirsh, Jr., chairman; Dr. Diane Ravitch, an author who was formerly with the U.S. Department of Education; Ms. Marion Joseph, a former member of the California State Board of Education; Mrs. E. D. (Polly) Hirsch; Ted Hirsch, assistant principal, South Shore Charter School; Louisa Spencer, retired attorney; Dr. Sandra Scarr, former president, KinderCare; Dr. William Moloney, superintendent, Colorado State Department of Education; Dr. James Cooper, University Of Virginia Curry School of Education; Ruth Wattenberg, American Federation of Teachers; and Robert Reid, director of the J. F. Maddox Foundation.

❖

Above: Core Knowledge Foundation's headquarters is located at 801 East High Street in Charlottesville and on the internet at www.coreknowledge.com.

Below: Barbara Garvin-Kester, president of Core Knowledge Foundation and former director of the Federal Executive Institute in Charlottesville, Virginia.

A recent article in *American Educator* magazine applauded the growth of Core Knowledge and said, "Inspired by the trenchant, insightful writings of E. D. Hirsch, Jr., and his unwavering and courageous determination to focus attention on the problems with the curriculum and the need to expose all children to a common core of rich subject matter, scores of teachers, parents, and administrators rallied to his common-sense ideas and worked to give them flesh."

The Core Knowledge curriculum has been successful with teachers, school administrators, and parents across the nation.

For example, in 1992, parents in Fort Collins, Colorado, petitioned the local school district for a different kind of public elementary school, one that would emphasize character education and parental involvement. But, most of all, it would emphasize a content-rich curriculum that would leave nothing to chance. The curriculum selected was the *Core Knowledge Sequence*. It has become so popular that the school teaching Core Knowledge now has a waiting list of more than two hundred students.

"We now know that a sequenced curriculum with rich and challenging content can work for all students, advantaged and disadvantaged alike," says Dr. Garvin-Kester. "We will continue to develop this curriculum and to find new ways of implementing it in many more schools. We will also find new ways of supporting our teachers in the field and tapping into their classroom experience as a way of improving our efforts. We will also reach out to educators who want to improve the preparation of teachers and to legislators and policy makers who want to influence the direction of American education, not with empty rhetoric, but with sound ideas and adequate funds."

The third United States President and Declaration of Independence author Thomas Jefferson's famed Virginia mountain estate, Monticello, is the only home in America on the elite *World Heritage List of the United Nations.* Approximately 500,000 guests visit this National Historic Landmark each year, and in 2004 it passed the 25 million mark in all-time public attendance.

Jefferson began clearing the land for Monticello in 1768 and started construction the following year. He sketched the drawings for the house himself and for over forty years he continued to be involved with its construction and expansion. The home was built from bricks made on-site and most of the structural timber came from Jefferson's land. The nails for remodeling were also crafted at Monticello and the stone for the cellars and columns, as well as the limestone used to make mortar, were quarried on his land as well.

Upon his return from Europe in 1789, where he served as U.S. minister to France, Jefferson started to redesign Monticello in a neoclassical style, compatible with the French taste of the time. Seven years later, he began to add new rooms and erected the famous dome over the center of the building. He made a myriad of other changes but due to his frequent extended absences, many were not completed until 1809. As late as 1825, the year before his death, Jefferson was still modifying Monticello.

Jefferson said of Monticello: "I am as happy no where else and in no other society, and all my wishes end, where I hope my days will end, at Monticello. Too many scenes of happiness mingle themselves with all the recollections of my native woods and fields, to suffer them to be supplanted in my affection by any other."

For more than eighty years Monticello has been owned and operated by the private, nonprofit Thomas Jefferson Foundation, which bought the property in 1923, after the federal government waived its third opportunity to acquire the estate. Its stewardship includes the 33-room house and gardens on nearly 2,000 of Jefferson's original 5,000 acres. Despite the fact that it receives no ongoing federal or state funding, it successfully maintains a twofold mission of preservation and education, providing a wide variety of community-based programming to the public, offering several different tours of Monticello, holding a range of special events throughout the year, and operating a host of entities including the Robert H. Smith International Center for Jefferson Studies, Jefferson Library, two Museum shops and a catalog, and the Monticello Visitors Center, which houses a permanent exhibition, theatre, and education center.

For more information on Monticello and the Thomas Jefferson Foundation, visit their website at www.monticelllo.org.

THOMAS JEFFERSON FOUNDATION

❖

Owned and operated since 1923 by the nonprofit Thomas Jefferson Foundation, Monticello is open to visitors every day of the year except Christmas.

COURTESY OF MONTICELLO/ THOMAS JEFFERSON FOUNDATION, INC.

ACAC FITNESS AND WELLNESS CENTERS

ACAC first opened its doors in 1984, in a small building on the corner of Hydraulic Road and 29 North. The original desire of founder and owner, Phil Wendel, was to provide a clean, well-equipped club where those who were passionate about fitness could work out. Within six months of opening, ACAC grew from a starting membership of 100 to nearly 400 initiated exercisers. With the original goal in sight, Wendel soon saw the need for a health club that would go beyond "preaching to the converted," one that would serve those who needed the support and lifestyle enhancements a true wellness center could provide. In the twenty years since, ACAC's membership has spiraled to over 11,000 members.

Throughout these years of struggle and accomplishment, ACAC has grown through its mission , innovative partnerships with medical institutions, becoming a venue for everything from charity balls to high school proms, and the daily business of helping thousands of members live active lives, have all made ACAC far more than "just a gym." Incorporating the latest research and technology into its programs and facility designs, ACAC remains on the cutting edge, expanding its facilities and offerings to meet the ever-changing needs of a diverse community.

A unique aspect of ACAC is its links to the medical community. These links include a physician referral program, a staff nurse, and an onsite physical therapy clinic, operated in conjunction with Martha Jefferson Hospital. Phil Wendel's heart is in his business, and he is passionate about the need for Americans to focus on preventative medicine.

"Sixty-one percent of Americans are now overweight and childhood obesity is on the rise. Research is proving beyond a shadow of a doubt that conditions such as diabetes, heart disease, stroke, and cancer are attributable in many cases to lifestyle factors," Wendel says. According to the World Health Organization, by the year 2020, these 'preventable' conditions will be responsible for seventy-five percent of deaths worldwide. "This is just tragic," says Wendel, "and yet it is also empowering, in that it tells people they have a chance to turn things around."

ACAC is built on this concept. "The answer in most cases is something as simple as fitness and good nutrition," he believes. "But it won't happen by offering a gym that appeals only to those who already exercise. We need to reach out to the general population and provide a place where members of all ages and abilities can feel comfortable, ask questions, explore fitness and find ways to make changes in their individual lives."

ACAC's growth and development has been driven by this overarching desire to change lives. Wendel recognizes there are many different ways of achieving fitness besides aerobics classes and free weights. ACAC programs cover a wide range of interests and skill levels and embrace the concept that health and wellness are not won by muscle alone. ACAC members participate in social activities, have an opportunity to try new sports and recreation, and discover unique forms of exercise.

To create its comprehensive fitness and wellness facilities, ACAC offers group exercise classes; body and mind classes including yoga, Pilates and Tai Chi; a full service spa; personal training; nutrition seminars and counseling; and an Active Aging seniors program. The AdventureZone introduces children to a healthful lifestyle while their parents work out. The HealthQuest area provides a supervised introduction to strength training and an express full-body circuit for those short on time. Aquatic facilities offer extensive water-based options and

have received top honors, ranking first in the state of Virginia for aquatic programs, and in the top twenty nationally for aquatic exercise. Not to be confined by four walls, ACAC's "discover" programs open the doors to white-water rafting, mountain biking, and rock climbing.

ACAC's main facility at Albemarle Square in Charlottesville offers such amenities as indoor pools, a karate school, day spa, and gymnasium. The Four Seasons location includes the ACAC WaterPark, a community sports arena, after-school programs, and summer camps and youth classes. A new downtown location on Monticello Avenue offers a comprehensive urban facility. ACAC sites are also thriving in West Chester, Pennsylvania, and Baltimore, Maryland.

The key to ACAC's success is its member service. ACAC believes in providing a sanctuary for wellness for each individual member. From the seventy-year-old focused on quality of life, to the five-year-old just learning to coordinate limbs and thoughts; from the twenty-five-year-old with a busy career and social life, to the forty-five-year-old in need of a fast and effective workout, ACAC lives up to its guiding principle: "We Change Lives!"

HAMPTON INN & SUITES AT THE UNIVERSITY

The warmth and charm of Charlottesville surrounds you as soon as you enter the lobby of the Hampton Inn & Suites at the University. Murals in the lobby depict such area attractions as the home of Thomas Jefferson, Monticello, James Madison's home, Montpelier, and the Rotunda at the University of Virginia.

Guests may choose from a variety of comfortable guest rooms and spacious suites.

Standard amenities in each room include high-speed internet access; twenty-five inch televisions with free HBO; two-line telephones with voicemail; clock radio; hairdryer, nightlight; and iron and ironing board.

Suites are fully equipped with two-burner stovetops, microwaves, dishwashers, and refrigerators with icemakers, a sofa bed, two televisions, and a DVD player. Some suites are available with cozy fireplaces.

In addition to the guest rooms, two meeting rooms are available at the Hampton Inn & Suites at the University.

The conference room seats up to thirty people and is perfect for training sessions, presentations, or small receptions. The room is tastefully decorated in the same rich tones as the lobby and is equipped with everything needed for a successful meeting. A television, DVD player, podium, flip chart, overhead projector, screen, and telephone are provided, as well as a data port that connects to free high speed Internet service.

The board room seats twelve people around a large walnut table with comfortable chairs and offers the same features as the conference room.

Catering services from local restaurants are available for either room.

In addition to the beautiful, comfortable guest rooms and well-equipped meeting

rooms, the Hampton Inn & Suites at the University offers complimentary transportation to and from the Charlottesville/ Albemarle Airport and the University of Virginia Medical Center.

Other amenities include a deluxe hot breakfast each morning, an on-site fitness room with aerobic equipment, and a complimentary on-site guest laundry.

Business services include fax, copies and Federal Express pick-up and delivery. Local calls are free and children under age eighteen may stay free in the same room with their parents.

The Hampton Inn & Suites at the University is located at 900 West Main Street in Charlottesville. You may phone them at 434-923-8600 or visit them on the Internet at www.hampsuites.com.

RIVANNA FARM

The majesty and grandeur of Old Virginia is preserved for future generations at Rivanna Farm, located on the north fork of the Rivanna River in scenic northeastern Albemarle County.

The land was home to generations of prominent Virginia families, including descendants of Thomas Jefferson. Their comfortable homes were showcases of antebellum charm and sophistication, their gardens a delight of color and expression. However, by 1957 only ruins and overgrown fields remained.

Above: The Upper South Terrace and South Wing.

Below: The main house.

Bottom: The main entrance gates and courtyard.

Rivanna Farm, consisting of 400 acres of open fields and pastures and 300 forested acres, was brought together in 1957 by Audrey Emery. The section west of the river was called Gale Hill and included remains of a 1760 home that burned in 1930. The portion of the farm east of the river also included the foundation of a burned home and this is where the farm's present manor house was built.

Emery used a local architect, Joe Norris, to design and build the new manor house with two adjacent wings around a cobblestone courtyard surrounded by a Jeffersonian wall. The estate is very European in appearance due to the influence of Emery's good friend, the French Count Pierre de Polignac, father-in-law of screen actress Grace Kelly.

The ground floor of the main house features an entrance hall with double-spiral staircase, a library, dining room, drawing room, kitchen, pantry and laundry. Upstairs are four bedrooms with four baths, and a boudoir and dressing room adjacent to the master bedroom. There also are four small, octagonal rooms in the Jefferson style and a large attic and basement. An elevator connects the floors.

The South Wing contains two bedrooms with three baths, and a large living room and a modern kitchen with dining area. All four rooms have open fireplaces.

In the North Wing are three bedrooms with two baths, an open fireplace in the hall, and a modern kitchen and laundry. The servants originally used this wing.

The gardens are on terraces on the south and west sides of the main house. There is also a beautiful rose garden, built up brick by brick to meet the level of

the west terrace. The iron works in the rose garden are of Gillette design. The half-mile-long entrance road was planted with pink flowering crabapple trees.

Emery sold the property to her nephew, Ethan Emery, who rebuilt part of the North Wing and installed a north-facing artist's studio.

The property was sold in 1974 to Carol and Paul Hoffman of Naperville, Illinois. The Hoffmans were collectors of modern art and displayed a large collection of photo-realist paintings and sculptures in the main house. They raised cattle and horses on the farm and installed a riding rink with obstacles.

In 1986 the Hoffmans sold the property to Swedish Count and Countess Archibald Douglas, then residing in Middleburg, Virginia, and they took over operation of the farm in May 1987. The Douglas' modernized the farm and restored the main house to its original beauty.

The makeover included restoration of the interiors, which had been designed for Emery by famous French interior designer Stephane Boudin of Jansen Company in Paris. Especially noteworthy are the walnut parquet floors throughout the house, the Chinese floral wallpapers in the dining room and eighteenth century mantelpieces of reddish Burgundy marble.

The Douglas family moved into Rivanna Farm in June 1991, and Margareta Douglas, now a widow, still resides there. Both wings were thoroughly modernized in 1997-98.

From 2000 to 2005, a professional gardener totally restored the gardens, using original plans from the Gillette drawings in the Library of Virginia in Richmond. Most of the property is under scenic easement with the Virginia Outdoors Foundation.

The rich history of the Trice family, which lived on the Gale Hill portion of Rivanna Farm, has been carefully researched and preserved in a professionally produced compact disk, *Trice Blessed*. The Trice family letters and genealogical research provide a rare glimpse of everyday life in the eighteenth and nineteenth centuries.

Above: A painting by Edward Thomas, February 1999.

Below: A color photo from 1994 before the houses were painted yellow with green shutters.

NAEVA Geophysics, Inc.

Above: The NAEVA Geophysics, Inc., headquarters in Charlottesville, Virginia.

Below: Dr. Robert S. Young, president of NAE from 1964 to 1979.

NAEVA Geophysics, Inc. is a small business service company, headquartered in Charlottesville, that conducts geophysical surveys for subsurface detection, primarily associated with environmental assessment and remediation. Geophysical methods employed in these investigations may include magnetics, electromagnetics, ground penetrating radar (GPR), seismic, resistivity, gravity, and borehole logging. Typical applications may include underground utility location, locating lost underground storage tanks and buried drums of potentially hazardous waste, and landfill investigations. NAEVA Geophysics has developed and demonstrated particular expertise at conducting digital geophysical mapping for locating potential unexploded ordnance (UXO) on active military bases or formerly used defense sites (FUDS).

NAEVA Geophysics, Inc. is a direct descendant of its former parent company, North American Exploration of Virginia (NAEVA), and prior to that, North American Exploration, Inc. (NAE). NAEVA Geophysics, Inc.'s mission is to be the leader in its field by providing quality services at competitive cost to the best companies in the environmental industry. To complete this mission, the company serves and satisfies its customers by continually striving to improve the quality of its products and services.

Dr. Robert S. Young, a native of Charlottesville, Virginia, founded the original parent company, NAE, in 1964. He held BA and

MA degrees from the University of Virginia and a Ph.D. in geology from Cornell University. During the period 1959-69, he served as assistant professor, associate professor, and assistant dean at the University of Virginia. Dr. Young was a distinguished expert in applying geochemistry, structural analysis, and geophysics to the field of mineral exploration for economic ore bodies. In 1964 he founded NAE as a consulting/service company to provide mineral exploration services to the mining industry. Early exploration projects included base and precious metal exploration in New England, the southeast, and the Great Basin of the western United States. These projects were followed by an extensive lignite coal exploration program in the Gulf Coast/Costal Plain of the southeastern United States on behalf of Phillips Petroleum Company. This was one of the largest mineral exploration programs ever conducted. Exploration holes were drilled every mile or two along a belt twenty to thirty miles wide from Texas to North Carolina.

In 1980, Dr. Young sold NAE to O. Jay Gatten, an independent consulting geologist from Kaysville, Utah and former executive with Phillips Petroleum Company. A western office of NAE was opened in Utah at that time, to offer similar mineral exploration field services to clients in the western states. In addition to the lignite coal exploration program in the early 1980s was an equally extensive oil shale exploration program for Phillips Petroleum Company in the central United States. Also, beginning in 1980, NAE embarked on a world-class diamond exploration program for Exmin Corporation of Bloomington, Indiana. Exploration services that NAE performed included geological mapping, geophysical surveying, and geochemical sampling throughout numerous states and provinces in the U.S. and Canada. This program lasted twenty years and was one of the largest "hardrock" mineral exploration programs ever conducted in the United States.

In 1993, NAE opened an office in Rockland County, New York, to perform subsurface detection services for environmental remediation and formed a subsidiary, North American Exploration of Virginia (NAEVA), which consisted of the Charlottesville and

New York offices. Both offices experienced slow but steady growth in the environmental geophysics field. In 1996, John Allan, an employee of twenty-one years, purchased NAEVA and renamed the company NAEVA Geophysics, Inc. in order to accent its focus on environmental geophysics.

Throughout the late 1990s and early 2000s NAEVA has experienced dramatic growth. A third office in Baltimore was opened in 2002, and the office facilities in New York doubled in size in 2003. Today, NAEVA Geophysics, Inc., with over thirty employees, has established itself as a national leader in the field of geophysical subsurface detection. The New York office has developed particular expertise in subsurface utility locating, even in ultracomplex environments like the streets of Manhattan. The Virginia office specializes in digital geophysical mapping on active or former military bases throughout the country and internationally. Such surveys typically detect potentially unexploded ordnance items (UXO) that may pose a threat to human safety. Programs of this nature have been carried out at Fort Ritchie, Fort Pickett, Fort Ord, Adak Island in Alaska, Camp Elliott, Aberdeen Proving Grounds, Fort Dix, Massachusetts Military Reservation, Hawaii, Vieques in Puerto Rico, and Bavaria, Germany.

Since 1996 the number of employees has tripled and revenues from environmental geophysical work have increased from $363,000 to over $3 million—almost ten fold! NAEVA is currently one of the largest employers of geologists and geophysicists in the State of Virginia, and historically, over the past forty years, has provided employment for hundreds of geologists.

NAEVA plans to continue its growth and expansion, and continue as the industry leader in performing subsurface detection geophysical surveys for environmental assessments.

For more information on NAEVA, please visit www.naevageophysics.com or contact President John D. Allan at (434) 978-3187, fax (434) 973-9791 or e-mail at jallan@naevageophysics.com.

Above: O. Jay Gatten, president of NAE/NAEVA from 1980 to 1995.

Bottom, left: John D. Allan, president of NAEVA Geophysics from 1996 to the present.

Bottom, right: NAEVA field personnel conducting a geophysical survey.

RICHARD A. OLIVA & SONS, INC.

An enduring art that has been admired for countless generations, the carving of marble and stone is an ancient skill that dates back to the beginning of time. It takes many years of training and painstaking practice to learn its finer points and carefully transform a slab of marble into an architectural work of art.

The dream of coming to America and discovering the opportunities available became a reality for Humbert Oliva at only eighteen years of age. A hard worker with characteristic determination, he emigrated from Italy and settled in the nation's capitol, Washington, D.C., where he learned ceramic tile and marble work. He journeyed south to Richmond, Virginia, in the mid-1920s to pursue work. There he met another tile setter, C. F. Lazzuri, and they established the firm Oliva & Lazzuri, Inc. in 1946.

Richard A. "Buster" Oliva, Humbert's son, joined his father in the business in June of 1949,

learning the trade as a tile setter in numerous locations around the Richmond area, and at the University of Virginia in Charlottesville. When the company decided to open a branch in the historic city, Buster agreed to become its director and moved his family there in 1955. When he bought the branch in 1978, Buster renamed the firm Richard A. Oliva & Sons, Inc., and its headquarters are located at 606 Tenth Street Northwest in Charlottesville.

Above: The offices of Richard A. Oliva & Sons are located at 606 Tenth Street, Northwest in Charlottesville.

Below: The company's fabrication shop.

At Richard A. Oliva & Sons, Inc., each work, from the simplest to the most complex, is carefully produced with the finest detail and greatest care by seventeen well-qualified employees. Craftsmen fabricate marble and granite in the company's facility at 1215 Five Springs Road, and install ceramic tile, marble, granite and limestone for high-end residential construction and commercial projects throughout the area.

Richard A. Oliva & Sons, Inc., has supplied ceramic tile and marble work for a number of well-known Charlottesville and Albemarle County businesses including the expansion of the old *Daily-Progress* newspaper building on Market Street and the old Citizens Bank on Main Street. The firm provided the tile and stone for the original Boar's Head Inn, was involved in the Farmington Country Club restoration, and recently helped with the restoration of the terrace at the University of Virginia Rotunda. In addition, the company has provided tile and terrazzo for many public schools in the area.

Today, Buster's sons—Michael, John and Donald—represent a third generation of Oliva craftsmanship in Virginia. Buster continues in his role as president of the company while Michael serves as vice president and director, John as its secretary and director, and Donald as its director.

Well-known for his skill, workmanship and honesty in the field, Buster was honored in 1976 to serve as "a committee of one" in selecting an appropriate stone on which to display the Daughters of the American Revolution plaque at the Albemarle County Courthouse. He located the pyramid-shaped rock on Monticello Mountain and transported it to the site.

Commenting on the company's achievements in Charlottesville over the past half-century, he says, "Our business is an art and we take pride that all of our people are trained here. Our goal remains to continue training highly skilled workmen who will be a credit to the profession and to maintain the high quality of workmanship and service established by our founder."

Having celebrated fifty years of the company's presence in Charlottesville in 2005, the Oliva family is honored to support the work of the Historical Society in preserving the area's unique and honorable history in Virginia.

Above: Richard A. Oliva & Sons supplied the slate wall cap for Peter Jefferson Place.

Below: Richard A. Oliva & Sons also provided the marble and slate for the University of Virginia's terrace renovation.

ALBEMARLE COUNTY

Albemarle County, located in the heart of the beautiful Blue Ridge Mountains, enjoys a rich heritage. The county was formed in 1744 and named after William Keppel, the second earl of Albemarle. Three U.S. presidents—Thomas Jefferson, James Monroe, and James Madison—called Albemarle County home, and Jefferson's home, Monticello, remains a popular historic attraction.

Albemarle County is composed of 725 square miles, surrounding the ten-square-mile City of Charlottesville. The county population is nearly 90,000 and the city's population approximately 41,000.

The University of Virginia, founded by Thomas Jefferson, plays a vital role in the community and provides outstanding educational and cultural resources.

The county is less than an hour's drive from the state capital in Richmond and close to such scenic attractions as the Blue Ridge Parkway, Skyline Drive and Shenandoah National Park. Six rivers—Rivanna, Moormans, Mechums, Hardware, Rockfish, and James—flow through the county.

Albemarle County is ideal for nature lovers. There are breathtaking views of mountains and valleys along the Skyline Drive and Blue Ridge Parkway, along with numerous trails for both casual and serious hikers. Dozens of parks, playgrounds and picnic areas provide plenty of recreational options for hikers, bikers, skiers, and fishermen.

The economy of Albemarle County is strong and stable. Agriculture and forestry are important aspects of the economy, with Albemarle County ranked twentieth among Virginia counties in the value of agricultural products sold. Over fifty percent of the county is forested and 9.9 million board feet of saw timber is harvested annually. Mineral production includes crushed stone, sand, and soapstone.

Albemarle County also enjoys a vibrant economy in such sectors as services, tourism, education, retail, travel, and trade. The county's unemployment rate is consistently lower than state and national averages.

A six-member board of supervisors representing each of the county's magisterial districts governs Albemarle County. A county executive, appointed by the board of supervisors, serves as the county's chief executive officer.

With a proud past and a promising future, Albemarle County is focused on preserving the scenic rural places that have always defined the community while creating quality spaces that provide convenient and attractive options for a more urban lifestyle.

For more information on beautiful Albemarle County, please visit them on the Internet at www.albemarle.org.

Few cities anywhere can offer their residents the combination of breathtaking scenery, small-town charm and urban sophistication found in Charlottesville.

Situated between the rolling Piedmont and awe-inspiring Blue Ridge Mountains, Charlottesville offers unlimited recreational opportunities, nationally recognized historical attractions, and a vigorous, modern economy.

Charlottesville is rich in political history. The city was organized as a planned community in 1762 and named in honor of Queen Charlotte, wife of England's King George III. Nearby are the homes of Thomas Jefferson, who drafted the Declaration of Independence and served as the third president; James Madison, author of the U.S. Constitution and the fourth president; and James Monroe, the nation's fifth president.

The city's historical Downtown Pedestrian Mall provides a unique blend of commercial, retail and residential spaces, and has been hailed by the nationally renowned Pew Partnership for Civic Change as a shining example of downtown revitalization. With a bustling business community, the development of two new theaters—Live Arts and the Paramount—and the on-going renovation of the Downtown Amphitheater, the Mall is poised to remain the economic, entertainment, and social center of the region for years to come.

Charlottesville is home to the highly respected University of Virginia, founded in 1819 by Thomas Jefferson, who was a Carlottesville resident at the time. The university's twelve thousand students, world-class faculty and championship football and basketball teams add immeasurably to the city's cultural and recreational offerings.

Charlottesville is also home to Piedmont Virginia Community College, a highly regarded public school system and a number of private/parochial schools. Charlottesville High School has been ranked as one of the top five hundred high schools in the nation for three consecutive years by *Newsweek* magazine.

In addition to education, the technology industry is a fast-growing sector in the local economy and efforts are currently underway to increase economic incentives for local technology companies. The University of Virginia invests more than $140 million annually for research and development, and a new Institute of Micro-Technology will incorporate leading technology into the workforce.

In addition to the University of Virginia, other major employers in the Charlottesville area include GE Fanuc, Inova Corporation, Lexis Publishing, Litton Sperry Marine, State Farm Insurance, Martha Jefferson Hospital, National Optronics, Pepsi Cola Bottling Company, SNL Securities, and Wachovia Bank.

It is no wonder that Charlottesville has been ranked as the number one place to live in America by such publications as *Frommer's Ranked and Rated* and *Money Magazine*. Charlottesville's list of accolades also includes "Best Golf Community for Retirees," "#1 Tennis Community," "Best Small Place for Business and Career," and "Best Small College Town."

For more information on what is available to you in Charlottesville, Virginia, please visit www.charlottesville.org.

CHASE INVESTMENT COUNSEL CORPORATION

Chase Investment Counsel Corporation started as a one-person operation in 1958 with $300,000 in assets under management and has grown to a 15-person firm which now manages $3.5 billion. It is the oldest independent registered investment adviser domiciled in Virginia.

The firm was founded by Derwood S. Chase, Jr., who became interested in investment counseling as a teenager under the tutelage of his father, who had been one of the first professional investment counselors in Chicago. While he was still an officer in the United States Air Force, Chase taught a number of evening adult education courses on investing. In fact, his very first client was a former student.

Chase, who grew up in Charlottesville, graduated from The University of Virginia and received his MBA from Harvard University before working briefly as an industry analyst for the Department of Commerce and then serving as a lieutenant in the U.S. Air Force.

"When the company started in 1958 we had a small office on Fifth Street Northeast and a part-time secretary," Chase recalls. "In 1980 we moved our offices to the current location at 300 Preston Avenue."

The company operated as a proprietorship of Derwood S. Chase, Jr. until 1964 when it was incorporated as Chase Investment Counsel Corporation.

Chase Investment Counsel now manages $3.5 billion in separate account assets for retirement, endowment, foundation, personal trusts, and individuals in thirty-two states. Through its two mutual funds it serves another 4,500 shareholders in 46 states.

By style, the firm emphasizes large-cap and mid-cap growth stocks, and manages equity and balanced separate accounts, as well as its large-cap growth mutual fund,

CHASX, and a mid-cap growth mutual fund, CHAMX.

The firm strives to achieve outstanding long-term investment results with a risk-averse approach by a team of five experienced investment professionals.

In selecting stocks, Chase Investment Counsel concentrates on equities of companies with "consistent earnings growth that sell at prudent prices." The firm believes in owning financially sound companies with a history of demonstrated earnings growth, without paying too much for that record of growth.

Assets under management have grown substantially in recent years. For example, in the year ending December 31, 2004, the firm's clients (separately managed accounts) increased by 19 percent and total assets by 40 percent.

Over the past three years, ending December 31, 2004, the firm's clients (separately managed accounts) increased 76 percent and total assets under management increased 169 percent.

Now in charge of a fifteen-person firm, with individual and institutional clients nationwide, Derwood S. Chase, Jr., stands with Senior Vice President David B. Scott.

Since the beginning of 2004 through December 31, 2005, the CHASX mutual fund grew 83 percent, to more than $220 million, and, in the past three years, its growth was 692 percent.

"We have been recognized by the *New York Times, Barron's, Value Line, Lipper, USA Today, Investor's Business Daily, Pensions & Investments* and *The Wall Street Journal* for our outstanding performance," comments Chase. "That recognition has been primarily responsible for our assets under management growth as various institutions (which now account for eighty percent of our assets) have discovered us. We've been able to attract and effectively serve some very demanding clients and their consultants."

Chase is a former governor of the Investment Counsel Association of America and a member of the New York and Richmond Societies of Financial Analysts. The firm has been active in Charlottesville civic affairs, through such organizations as Junior Achievement, Rotary International, the American Cancer Society Relay for Life, the Boys and Girls Club, and the Charlottesville/Albemarle Symphony Orchestra Society.

Chase Investment Counsel believes it is in a unique position to manage investments, with its process-oriented approach that has proven effective for over forty years. It combines fundamental, quantitative and technical research. With its moderate size, Chase Investment Counsel responds to the changing market conditions and effectively invests in a broader group of large and mid-cap growth companies without the marketability constraints of larger firms.

For additional information about Chase Investment Counsel Corporation, please visit www.chaseinv.com.

Above: In a one-person office, Derwood S. Chase, Jr. launches his career in investment counsel.

Below: Chase Investment Counsel Corporation has hosted its Annual Client Conference in Charlottesville since 1973. This particular photo was taken at Farmington Country Club, a frequent host for the event.

ALLIED CONCRETE COMPANY

Allied Concrete Company of Charlottesville dates its beginnings to 1945 when C. Wilson McNeely, Jr., an ambitious young man who had graduated from the School of Architecture at The University of Virginia only two years before, established a concrete block manufacturing firm known as Allied Supply.

The family owned business is now in its third generation and has grown to become one of the largest manufacturers and suppliers of ready-mix concrete, concrete block, and concrete-related building materials in central Virginia.

The first concrete blocks produced by Allied were made by hand in wooden molds. These blocks were used to construct a building to house a more modern automated block-making machine producing three blocks at a time in a matter of seconds.

Concrete block was in big demand during the construction boom that followed WWII and Allied Supply soon began to prosper. Ready-mix concrete production was added in 1952 and the company name was changed to Allied Concrete Company in 1965 to better represent the growing number of products offered by the firm. Tools for masonry and concrete finishing, bagged mortar and cement, brick and chimney supplies were all available at the Charlottesville location.

An automated central ready-mix plant was installed in Charlottesville in 1981, providing Allied with the ability to produce quality concrete at a much faster rate. New batch computers had the ability to store hundreds of mix designs and job-specific information essential in the production and delivery of the perishable product. Large concrete pours for the state, University of Virginia, and other commercial jobs demanded multiple trucks on the job at once and quick delivery was a must as Charlottesville began to grow rapidly.

Allied opened its second ready-mix production facility in Green County in 1991 to serve the growing Route 29 North corridor from Albemarle to Madison County. A concrete products and masonry sales center for this area was built shortly afterward to accommodate the needs of masons and concrete finishers, as well as homeowners.

Allied began a large growth spurt as sales centers began to provide more landscaping design and homeowner-related concrete products. Decorative colored and stamped concrete accompanied by concrete retaining wall block and paving products were a perfect complement to any home. The introduction of insulated concrete forms in the commercial and residential building business created another great outlet for ready-mix where concrete was being used throughout the entire building process in walls and above-grade floor slabs.

A third ready-mix plant was built in 1999 near the Interstate 64 and Route 15 intersection

in Louisa to provide sufficient coverage of the growth east of Albemarle County. A sales center was added at this location in 2004. This led to Allied's next expansion in 2002 when it acquired C. R. Butler Concrete and Building Supply in Orange County. Butler was another long time family-owned business and a great fit for Allied, bridging gaps between its existing operations. Allied was now able reach areas that were growing as a result of the building boom in northern Virginia. Culpepper, in particular, had a strong demand for concrete to handle massive residential development and Allied responded with the construction of a new ready-mix plant in 2004.

Today, Allied has a total of 175 employees company wide and was the first concrete producer to become S.H.A.R.P.S. certified, a

designation issued for full compliance with OSHA safety regulations and outstanding safety records. Owned by a family in its third generation, there is a strong focus at Allied on taking care of its employees and empowering them to make decisions. This has resulted in a low employee turnover rate and a large number of long-term employees and giving the company greater ability to support the growing communities from all locations.

The company's success ultimately depends on the community, and this has been recognized by Allied by donations of material and/ or funding to established local charities, nonprofit organizations and The University of Virginia.

HOSPICE OF THE PIEDMONT

The road traveled by those with a life-limiting illness can be difficult and lonely. It is a journey undertaken reluctantly, with little knowledge of what lies ahead and, ultimately, may involve more than the patient and family can handle alone.

Since 1980, Hospice of the Piedmont has shared these journeys with thousands of patients and their families throughout central Virginia. Firmly established as an essential resource in end-of-life care in the region, Hospice of the Piedmont is recognized as a leader in meeting the needs of patients with a life-limiting illness and empowering those who love and care for them.

With a reputation for excellence, the agency is an acknowledged expert in symptom control and pain management, sharing patient journeys by delivering highly personalized comfort care, while providing compassionate presence and support for the patient's loved ones. This partnership with patients and their families sets hospice apart in the healthcare system. Beyond caring for the physical needs of the patient, careful attention is given, at every stage of the journey, to the practical, emotional, spiritual, and bereavement needs of the entire family.

The impetus that led to the founding of Hospice of the Piedmont can be traced back to an address at the University of Virginia by Dame Cicely Saunders on October 4, 1978. The founder of St. Christopher's Hospice in London,

Dr. Saunders is widely recognized as "the mother of the modern hospice movement." Inspired by her address, a group of citizens began to explore the possibility of providing a hospice program for Charlottesville and surrounding counties. Among those responsible for the founding of Hospice of the Piedmont, three names stand out: Adge Coburn, Dr. George Cooper, and Dr. William Sandusky. Under their leadership, a group of interested persons was enlisted and, by the fall of 1980, the newly incorporated Hospice of the Piedmont was ready to accept its first patient. Dr. Cooper, then head of Radiology at the University of Virginia, became the first president of the Board of Directors and remained actively interested until his death in 1999.

Initially located on Sycamore Street in a small house owned by Martha Jefferson Hospital, the hospice, with the help of the Perry Foundation, moved into a two-story Victorian house on East Jefferson in the fall of 1987. Gradually outgrowing that facility, the hospice moved into an office building on North Twenty-Ninth, in August 1994 and, in April 1999, relocated to a new medical building in the Pantops area where Martha Jefferson Hospital had agreed to lease space for the agency's offices. Finally, with the pressing need for additional space, the offices were relocated to 2200 Old Ivy Road in April 2004.

Patients receive personal care from the many healthcare professionals at Hospice of the Piedmont.

Since 1988, Hospice of the Piedmont has been certified to provide service under the Hospice Medicare Benefit and, responding to the need for hospice care in areas without a Medicare certified hospice, the original service area of Charlottesville and five counties now encompasses nine counties in central Virginia—Albemarle, Augusta, Buckingham, Fluvanna, Greene, Madison, Lousia, Nelson and Orange.

Care is provided by interdisciplinary teams of healthcare professionals made up of registered nurses, nurse's aides, social workers, chaplains and trained volunteers. For those patients who no longer live in their own homes, the services of Hospice of the Piedmont extend to assisted living facilities, nursing homes, the Hospice House that opened in 2004 and other facilities where patients reside.

Beyond these comprehensive services for the terminally ill and their families, Hospice of the Piedmont provides, as a public service, a Transitions program for prehospice patients, the Journeys art therapy program for children and teens who have lost a loved one, and bereavement counseling and support for anyone in their service area who is dealing with the loss of a loved one.

Above: Hospice House Residence.

Below: Participants from a Journeys camp for children and parents.

ALBEMARLE CHARLOTTESVILLE HISTORICAL SOCIETY

Mission Statement

The Albemarle Charlottesville Historical Society nurtures and promotes awareness and appreciation of local history by encouraging the identification, collection, study, and preservation of the materials of history; by striving for excellence and quality in research and interpretation of collections and local history; and by disseminating knowledge through educational activities, so that the past may shed light on the present and the future.

Activities toward which the efforts of the Albemarle Charlottesville Historical Society are directed include but are not limited to:

Encouraging the collection and preservation of manuscript and printed materials and other physical remains pertaining to the history of Charlottesville and Albemarle County;

Promoting historical programs, lectures, exhibitions, and other educational activities;

Facilitating writing and reporting upon local history in its relation to the local community, the Commonwealth of Virginia, the Nation, and foreign countries; and

Exhibiting such material in its own or other museums or elsewhere and maintaining and operating a library and museum for housing and displaying historic materials.

The Albemarle Charlottesville Historical Society is a private, non-profit educational organization (I.R.S. 501 (c) 3). The Society is a membership organization, open to all, and receives no continuing operating support from federal, state or local governments. We operate thanks to membership fees, gifts and donations, project grants from private foundations, and investments earnings from a small endowment.

Founded in 1940, the Albemarle Charlottesville Historical Society seeks to study, preserve, and promote the history of Charlottesville and Albemarle County, Virginia. The Society strives to accomplish this mission through a variety of public programs, including exhibits, publications, lectures, walking tours, oral history interviews, and various educational programs.

The Society's research library contains over two thousand books and bound periodicals, as well as thousands of photographs, manuscripts, maps, pamphlets, newspapers, and vertical files relating to the history of our community. The Society's museum collection contains over fifteen hundred artifacts of historical significance to Charlottesville and Albemarle County.

The Albemarle Charlottesville Historical Society is located in downtown Charlottesville in the historic McIntire Building. The McIntire Building, designed in the Beaux Arts style by architect Walter Dabney Blair, was completed in 1921 and donated to the City of Charlottesville as the city's first municipal library by local civic benefactor Paul Goodloe McIntire.

The Society, formerly located at 220 Court Square, completed an extensive renovation of the city-owned building in 1993 and moved into its new quarters in January 1994.

For information on all the Society's programs, meetings and tours; membership and donation support; hours of operation, research links and current news; and to see on-line versions of some recent exhibits, please visit our website at www.albemarlehistory.org.

Situated on a picturesque 573-acre estate boasting gently rolling hills, idyllic ponds, and tranquil meadows, Boar's Head Inn is nestled in the foothills of the Blue Ridge Mountains, just two miles from downtown Charlottesville and the University of Virginia. This AAA Four-Diamond classic country resort features an authentic early nineteenth century gristmill as its centerpiece, complemented by modern amenities and conveniences, stunning scenery and gracious hospitality. From fine dining to a state-of-the-art sports club, a luxury spa, championship golf, expansive tennis, and swimming facilities to outstanding conference and meeting rooms, Boar's Head Inn promises all guests a rewarding and memorable experience. Boar's Head was originally the site of Terrell's Ordinary, a modest inn built in the 1730s where westward travelers would stop to rest for the night. By the 1960s the Ordinary was long gone but it sparked an idea among a group of local businessmen to create the quintessential Virginia inn on the same site. So when Inn founder John Rogan discovered the ruins of an 1834 gristmill along the banks of the Hardware River, he saw an opportunity to preserve and transform a historic artifact. The mill had survived the burning ordered by Generals Grant and Custer during their Civil War march through Charlottesville and had continued to operate for sixty years after the war's end before it was finally abandoned. Each piece of the mill was painstakingly numbered and dismantled and was carefully reconstructed on the present site of the Inn. Boar's Head Inn was purchased in 1988 by the University of Virginia Foundation. Since that time, the University of Virginia Foundation has invested almost $30 million to renovate and continually upgrade the Inn. Among the foundation's most recent efforts are the 2005 renovations of Birdwood Golf Course and the Sports Club, which transformed these facilities into arguably the finest on the East Coast.

The original fieldstone, heart pine beams, planks, and massive grist stones are now prominently featured throughout the Inn and the gristmill itself is home to the Old Mill Room. This acclaimed restaurant has earned the coveted AAA Four-Diamond rating for over seventeen consecutive years and in 2002 was named the Virginia Wine Restaurant of the Year. Today Boar's Head Inn is a charming retreat offering 159 guest rooms and eleven suites, all of which boast luxury bedding, voice-mail telephone services, high speed Internet access, cable television, a personal safe, iron and ironing board, hair dryer, mini refrigerator, and coffeemaker. The Inn's recreational activities include the par-seventy-two Birdwood Golf Course; luxurious Boar's Head Spa; a state-of-the-art Sports Club featuring twenty-six tennis courts, three swimming pools, two squash courts, and a host of exercise classes and fitness equipment. In addition, Boar's Head offers complimentary bicycles and fishing poles, a kid's club, and hot air ballooning,

Boar's Head Inn, a country resort at the University of Virginia, is a delightful, well-appointed haven located in the crown jewel of the Virginia Commonwealth. They invite you to sample their gracious hospitality and lovely mountain setting. For more information visit them on the Internet at www.boarsheadinn.com or call 1-800-476-1988.

Beautiful rooms and stunning scenery are only the beginning of what awaits you at Boar's Head Inn.

CARLISLE MOTION CONTROL INDUSTRIES, INC.

For more than sixty years, Carlisle Motion Control Industries has led the heavy-duty trucking industry by offering innovative brake products and responsive customer service. The company has expanded its product line to include a wide variety of application-specific friction materials and brake shoe remanufacturing. Carlisle continues to build on its heritage of commitment to world-class quality and its customer-first focus.

Carlisle Motion Control Industries, an ISO 9001-certified company, manufactures heavy-duty brake linings, disc brake linings, brake shoe remanufacturing and relining for on-highway Class 6, 7, and 8 trucks. The company markets its products to heavy-duty truck and trailer OE manufacturers, brake and axle manufacturers, and to end-use fleets through aftermarket distribution.

The demands placed on heavy-duty braking systems have never been greater. Improved vehicle aerodynamics, pressure to reduce maintenance costs, and improper use of air brake systems by drivers increase stress on vehicle brakes. To meet the technological requirements of today's brake systems, Carlisle built a twenty-five-thousand-square-foot research and development facility in Charlottesville. The company chose to build its new facility here in part to establish a cooperative material study research arrangement with the University of Virginia.

The company's research and development initiatives focus on product innovation, including development of next-generation brake linings. Carlisle Motion Control works to improve product quality by providing a seamless interface between manufacturing and R&D.

In addition to its Charlottesville technical center, Carlisle Motion Control operates two friction-manufacturing plants in Virginia, a distribution center, and three brake shoe remanufacturing facilities.

Carlisle Motion Control Industries is a division of Carlisle Companies Incorporated, founded in 1917 by Charles S. Moomy as the Carlisle Tire and Rubber Company in Carlisle, Pennsylvania. The company's original purpose was to sell inner tubes to Montgomery Ward and Company. Since that time, Carlisle's diversification efforts, through both product line extensions and acquisitions, have resulted in a market-leading company with an enduring competitive advantage.

For more information and location of Carlisle Motion Control Industries, visit them on the Internet at www.carlislemotion.com.

Friction Brake Linings.

Founded in 1882, Richmond & Fishburne, L.L.P. has provided quality legal services to the Charlottesville, Albemarle County and Virginia community for over a century.

Former Charlottesville Mayor Daniel Harman established the firm at 0 Court Square in Charlottesville as a sole practitioner with quill and pad. Providing legal services under several generations of different firm names, Richmond & Fishburne took its current name in 1966 in recognition of its distinguished senior partners, Joseph W. Richmond and Junius R. Fishburne.

Today the firm has relocated to a newer Court Square location and uses the latest technology and equipment to provide cost effective, quality representation for its clients. The firm's practice areas include wealth and estate planning, trust and estate administration, elder law, real estate, business and civil litigation. Its client base includes individuals and businesses throughout Virginia. The firm's website is www.richfish.com.

Members of the firm have been recognized in *Best Lawyers in America* and *Virginia's Best Lawyers* and have qualified as board certified trial advocates. They have held offices in local, state and national professional associations. They are frequent presenters at continuing legal education seminars and other programs for attorneys and others throughout the state, and are authors and editors of various articles and legal publications.

Through the years, members of the firm have held leadership in local and state organizations, including president of the Virginia State Bar, mayor of Charlottesville, chairman of the Charlottesville Regional Chamber of Commerce, and Virginia State Delegate and Senator. They have served on

Daniel Harman - Founder

Daniel Harman · 1882-1906
Harman & Walsh · 1907-1920
Allen, Walsh & Michie · 1921-1925
Allen & Walsh · 1926-1928
Allen, Walsh & Waddell · 1928-1932
Walsh & Waddell · 1933-1944
Walsh, Waddell & Coles · 1945-1946
Waddell & Coles · 1947-1950
Waddell, Coles & Richmond · 1950-1951
Coles & Richmond · 1951-1956
Richmond & Via · 1957-1964
Richmond, Via & Fishburne · 1964-1965

Richmond and Fishburne · 1966-

boards of charitable and other nonprofit organizations and have provided pro bono legal services to citizens who otherwise would be denied legal representation. The American Red Cross, United Way, Jefferson Area Board for Aging, Martha Jefferson Hospital and Rotary have all benefited from the participation of the firm's members on their governing boards and committees. Members of the firm have been involved in the formation of several elder care communities in central Virginia, including Westminster-Canterbury of the Blue Ridge and Mountainside Senior Living.

The firm's current attorneys include Joseph W. Richmond, Jr., Wendall L. Winn, Jr., Matthew B. Murray, Christine Thomson, Joseph M. Cochran, Mark J. Nelson, Richard Armstrong, Marcelle Morel and J. Walker Richmond III. These attorneys and their successors will continue to provide Virginia with quality legal services in the years to come.

RICHMOND & FISHBURNE, L.L.P.

Left: The original offices at 0 Court Square in Charlottesville.

STEVENS & COMPANY

The long tradition of honesty and professionalism begun in 1938 by William T. Stevens continues today at Stevens & Company under the direction of Flip Faulconer.

Stevens, a Central Virginia native, sold significant Virginia estates for more than fifty-five years, bringing to each transaction his unique reverence and stewardship of the area. Perhaps his proudest achievement was selling four presidential landmarks in one year. At the age of eighty-two, Stevens could still be found doing what he loved most, marketing this beautiful and historic area.

Flip Faulconer, who purchased Stevens & Company in 1990, left her career as a buyer for Bonwit Teller in New York to become the owner of two women's specialty shops in Charlottesville. She later joined her husband, Hunter, in real estate and brings more than two decades of local real estate experience to each transaction.

Faulconer continues the Stevens brand of real estate brokerage typified by the highest professional standards and unparalleled local market knowledge, combined with an intimate appreciation of what makes our area so special.

In addition to residential Charlottesville properties, Stevens & Company specializes in farms, estates, country properties, retreats, and land throughout the Virginia Piedmont and greater Central Virginia areas.

Stevens & Company often features luxury estates and other fine and historic properties outside the town of Charlottesville; in Albemarle, Greene, Orange, Nelson, Madison, Fluvanna, Amherst, and Culpepper Counties; in and around Fredericksburg, Ivy, Warrenton, Afton, Barbourseville, Rapidan, Gordonsville, Crozet, Free Union, Earlysville, White Hall, and Greenwood; on or near the country clubs of Farmington, Keswick, and Glenmore; and in close proximity to the University of Virginia, Ashlawn-Highland, Montpelier, and Monticello.

Stevens & Company is headquartered at One Boar's Head Place in Charlottesville. You may view current listings on the Internet at www.stevensandcompany.net.

In 1948, Robert W. Mincer concluded his position as the foreman of a pipe factory that had just been sold in Long Island, New York. During his early tenure in the tobacco industry, Mincer took note of the popularity of pipes and tobacco among the servicemen returning from WWII. Mincer decided it would be a lucrative venture to open a pipe shop in a college town where his intended customers were plentiful.

After much research and forethought, the entrepreneur decided to base his new business in Charlottesville, Virginia. Mincer's Humidor opened its doors for business on July 19, 1948. The tiny, 217 square-foot shop was located in a space that is now under the stairwell of Michael's Bistro on the UVA Corner. Robert and his wife, Clara, diligently worked together in the pipe shop establishing a tradition that would continue for generations of University students and supporters.

As the pipe shop prospered, Mincer's Humidor moved to its current location at 1527 University Avenue in the summer of 1954 to accommodate the growth. With the move, the business would also receive the new name of Mincer's Pipe Shop. Besides pipes and tobacco products, a substantial selection of books, greeting cards, and magazines were also stocked in the store, supplying many of the needs of students at the time. In addition to these changes, the pipe shop also welcomed a new generation of the Mincer family. Robert Mincer's son, Robert H. "Bobby" Mincer, graduated from the McIntire School of Commerce at the University of Virginia in 1958 and joined the family business full-time in 1960.

The 1960s and 1970s entailed more changes for the family-owned business. As traditions and trends began to evolve at the University, the Mincers decided to experiment and make modifications in their merchandise. At one time,

Mincer's Pipe Shop was the largest record dealer between Washington, D.C., and Raleigh, North Carolina. The store's stationery supply was also in high demand before the days of e-mail and inexpensive long-distance phone calls. School spirit began to soar in the 1970s as various athletic teams became more successful in collegiate sports. Students began to replace the once customary formal attire of "coat and tie" with the more casual choice of Mincer's University of Virginia apparel to show their school support.

During the 1980s, Bobby's son, Mark, became more involved in the family business. Mark chose to continue his family's tradition upon his graduation from the School of Commerce in 1985. With a new generation prepared to operate the business, the Mincers decided to renovate the store and enlarge it to its current size.

As the demand for tobacco and tobacco products declined due to trends and health concerns, Mincer's Pipe Shop phased out its tobacco business. Reacting to customer demands, the store began to specialize in apparel, accessories, and gifts decorated with UVA logos. The shop's name was changed to Mincer's University of Virginia Imprinted Sportswear. With its prominent location "right on the corner of The Corner," Mincer's is packed with students, parents and fans before athletic and academic events. In recent years, an increasing portion of business has come through Internet sales. A full line of merchandise may be viewed and ordered online at www.mincers.com.

"We have been successful because we were willing to try new things and go with the trends," comments Mark. "Being a third-generation, family-operated business has certainly been one of our most important assets."

Left: Mincer's offers hundreds of various University of Virginia items including over fifty different sweatshirts. A large selection of apparel, accessories, and gifts is offered on the company's website at www.mincers.com.

Below: Mincer's has been located on the corner of The Corner at 1527 University Avenue since the summer of 1954.

OUR LADY OF PEACE

In 1983, Ruth DePiro, a member of Holy Comforter Church, inquired of Father Carl Naro about Catholic-sponsored housing for the elderly in the Charlottesville area.

After some research, Father Naro provided Ruth DePiro with information concerning other housing projects for seniors in which the Diocese was involved. Shortly after the inquiry, a Board of Directors was established in 1984 with Ruth DePiro as the president.

Groundbreaking for Our Lady of Peace was conducted on a beautiful Sunday afternoon, September 15, 1991. Bishop Walter F. Sullivan presented the keynote address, praising the dedicated individuals whose hard work made Our Lady of Peace a reality for the senior population and applauded their vision of an affordable retirement community.

The retirement community was originally called Moore House in honor of Father Bernard Moore, whose foresight prompted the purchase of a tract of land near the Church of the Incarnation off Route 29 North in Charlottesville. The name was later changed to Our Lady of Peace to better reflect its focus as a middle-income residential community and to reflect its identification with the Catholic Church.

Our Lady of Peace, a caring retirement community, is located at 751 Hillsdale Drive in Charlottesville. The nonprofit, nondenominational retirement community offers independent, assisted living, nursing care and a specialized dementia care unit. A full schedule of recreational, social, and religious activities, housekeeping, gracious dining, transportation, and around-the-clock nursing care are just a few of the amenities provided for residents.

Our Lady of Peace is one of eleven Diocesan owned and operated senior communities in Virginia. Other facilities are located in Virginia Beach, Richmond, Lynchburg, Roanoke, and Hampton.

As head of the Catholic Diocese of Richmond, Bishop Sullivan was involved in promotion of elderly housing for more than twenty years. "I believe it's the role of the church to reach out to a group of people that are forgotten or ignored," he says. "I am firmly committed to congregate living, where people will not live in isolation, but share life together as a family."

Bishop Sullivan retired in June 2004 and now serves as bishop emeritus.

Additional information about Our Lady of Peace may be found on the Internet at www.our-lady-of-peace.com.

Above: The main lobby at Our Lady of Peace.

Below: Our Lady of Peace Retirement Community.

Hantzmon Wiebel is one of the oldest firms in Charlottesville and, as its leading CPA firm, touches most sectors of the local economy.

Hantzmon Wiebel dates from 1928 when R. G. Hantzmon, a young accountant for a Washington, D.C., firm, came to Charlottesville to audit a local company. He decided to stay and open his own practice. In 1941, Reuel Wiebel, Jr., joined the firm, and in 1956 the firm began using both names. Hantzmon's son, Van, served the firm for approximately forty-five years. Now owned and operated by ten partners, the firm celebrated its first seventy-five years of service to Central Virginia in 2003.

Hantzmon Wiebel is unusual among Charlottesville companies in that its ownership and structure have changed little during its history. Never bought or sold or merged with another firm, the company has grown internally to meet the demands of the area, operating in the same unassuming brick building at 818 East Jefferson Street since 1962.

While maintaining a low profile and keeping its focus on Central Virginia, Hantzmon Wiebel has grown to become, in 2004, the sixth largest Virginia-based CPA firm. Most of the firm's 2,500 clients—ranging from individuals and small businesses to multimillion dollar international firms—are located within a 100-mile radius of Charlottesville. Despite this regional focus, Hantzmon Wiebel is highly respected across the state and enjoys a growing national reputation. Many of the partners and several managers have been cited in *Virginia Business* magazine as "Super CPAs."

Hantzmon Wiebel actively participates in many community organizations. In addition to financial contributions and a philanthropic Education Fund, the firm supports local groups through volunteer activities ranging from board memberships to hands-on work in the United Way's Day of Caring. Hantzmon Wiebel greatly appreciates and proudly serves Charlottesville and Central Virginia.

For more information on Hantzmon Wiebel, please visit www.hantzmonwiebel.com.

❖

Above: Hantzmon Wiebel, Certified Public Accountants, has been an integral part of the Albemarle-Charlottesville community since 1928. Located in downtown Charlottesville on East Jefferson Street, the firm prides itself on client service and technical excellence, working with individuals, businesses, and nonprofit organizations.

Below: Hantzmon Wiebel is Central Virginia's largest certified public accounting firm, serving Charlottesville-Albemarle since 1928. In addition to professional audit, accounting, trust and estate work, and tax services, the firm has developed multiple technical niches, including employee benefit plans, tax-exempt organizations, multistate businesses, and business valuations.

McLean Faulconer, Inc.

McLean Faulconer, Inc., was founded in 1980 with the goal of providing the highest professional services available for its clients and customers. Since that beginning, McLean Faulconer has become the leading real estate firm for the marketing and sale of fine residential and estate properties in Charlottesville and Central Virginia.

Charlottesville natives Stephen T. McLean and James W. Faulconer, Jr., both of whom have been active in the local real estate business since 1974, organized the firm.

McLean Faulconer's main focus is the sale of luxury residences and estates, equestrian properties, farms, manor homes, country estates, and large land packages. The firm has also been involved in the listing and/or sale of many of the area's residential, commercial, farm and estate properties.

The more than twenty-five licensed real estate professionals at McLean Faulconer provide a diverse background of expertise in such fields as marketing, architecture, construction, landscape architecture, urban planning, historic preservation, general contracting, forestry, state government, and community service.

Many of the agents grew up in the Charlottesville/Albemarle County area and are active in a wide variety of community activities. Their familiarity with the area enables them to place the right prospect with the right home in as short a period of time as possible.

McLean Faulconer, Inc. is committed to protecting our rural areas through the promotion of conservation easements. The preservation of open land greatly enhances the lifestyle and atmosphere of this traditional area that Thomas Jefferson spoke so endearingly of when he said: "The situation of Charlottesville is in a mountainous, healthy, fertile country, delicious climate…good society and free as the air in religion and politics; come then my dear sir, to see this place." We feel the same about the Charlottesville of today.

In addition to Charlottesville and Albemarle County, McLean Faulconer lists and sells real estate properties in the surrounding Central Virginia Counties of Madison, Orange, Greene, Fluvanna, Louisa, Nelson, and Augusta, as well as in the Shenandoah Valley and Lexington areas.

For a preview of McLean Faulconer's wide range of properties, please browse through the current property listings at www.mcleanfaulconer.com or stop by the firm's office at 503 Faulconer Drive, Suite Five in Charlottesville, Virginia.

W. A. LYNCH ROOFING COMPANY, INC.

Few businesses in the Charlottesville area are as well known and respected as W. A. Lynch Roofing Company, Inc. Since its beginning in 1953, the company has been committed to providing superior products and the highest level of construction services to its customers. The firm was organized and founded by William A. Lynch, Sr., who had previously gained experience as a partner in Blue Ridge Insulation and Roofing Company from 1940 until 1953.

Today the business continues to successfully serve the roofing needs of Virginia and beyond. The company still accepts the challenge of combining the finest materials with the foremost craftsmen in the roofing industry to meet the needs of its clients. W. A. Lynch Roofing specializes in commercial, industrial and institutional roofing as well as specialty sheet metal applications and high-end residential roofing.

The principals are William A. Lynch, Jr., and Thomas F. McGraw III. Together they have maintained the company's high standards while successfully growing the business. The company's satisfied client list is long and distinguished. From the University of Virginia to GE, from Human Genome Sciences to many of Albemarle County's finest estates, the same quality and excellence is maintained for jobs big and small.

"We have very little turnover," says Lynch. "The average tenure for our employees is over seventeen years. This experience and dedication to quality work has led to our success." Vice President Thomas McGraw has been with the firm since 1975. Senior project manager Jack Masloff has been with the company since 1985. Lynch's son, Darren, representing the third generation, is also a project manager with the firm.

In the year 2000, Lynch and McGraw started W. A. Lynch Roofing Company of Lynchburg, Virginia, to expand the company's geographic capabilities. With over thirty employees, this office follows the same business model as the Charlottesville office; offering customers the finest materials installed by a well trained and experienced workforce.

❖

Above: Terne coated stainless steel roofing at the University of Virginia School of Law.

Below: Spanish tile roofing at an Albemarle County residence.

MCGUIREWOODS
LLP

❖

Egbert Watson.

In 1834 a twenty-four-year-old University of Virginia graduate, Egbert Watson, began practicing law in Charlottesville. More than 170 years later, the law practice he set in motion has grown into McGuireWoods LLP, one of the nation's largest law firms, with more than 750 lawyers in 14 offices in the United States, Europe and Central Asia.

Since its founding, McGuireWoods has maintained a location in the historic Charlottesville-Albemarle Court Square, within walking distance of Watson's original office.

The firm's Charlottesville office offers sophisticated business, labor and employment, creditor's rights, real estate, tax, and estate planning services. Clients include small businesses and publicly held companies, partnerships, limited liability companies, and individuals. McGuireWoods handles commercial, labor and employment, and tort litigation in federal and state courts throughout the Southeast. The office also has an active practice in the areas of healthcare and exempt organizations, representing both individual and corporate healthcare providers, as well as important regional and national private foundations and educational institutions.

The broad and dynamic approach to the practice of law that characterizes the present firm can be traced back to many significant mergers and leading individual partners including Watson, who read law under former President James Monroe, and whose career included six years in the Virginia General Assembly and as a circuit court judge.

By 1936, one hundred years after its beginnings, Watson's firm had evolved into Perkins, Battle, and Minor, and included among its members a future Virginia governor and a grandson of John B. Minor, longtime professor at the University of Virginia Law School and the author of *Minor's Institutes*, an ambassador to Australia, and a commissioner of the Internal Revenue Service.

In the years since, the firm, which became McGuireWoods in 2000, has opened many offices and merged with dynamic local law firms. It now has offices in Atlanta, Baltimore, Charlotte, Charlottesville, Chicago, Jacksonville, New York, Norfolk, Pittsburgh, Richmond, Tysons Corner, and Washington, D.C., as well as Brussels, Belgium, and Almaty, Kazakhstan.

One of the most prominent law firms in the world, McGuireWoods is able to offer sophisticated legal services throughout the market areas of the firm's many offices by utilizing twenty-first century technology from its Charlottesville Court Square office

For more information, please contact R. Craig Wood, Charlottesville office managing partner at the Court Square Building, 310 Fourth Street Northeast, Suite 300, Charlottesville, Virginia 22902-1288; or by telephone at 434-977-2558, by fax at 434-980-2274 or by email at cwood@mcguirewoods.com. Additionally, you may read more about McGuireWoods on the Internet at www.mcguirewoods.com.

RESIDENCE INN BY MARRIOTT

Residence Inn by Marriott opened in Charlottesville in 1997 and promptly received the Opening Hotel of the Year Award, the gold Hotel Award and General Manager of the Year Award.

In the years since, Residence Inn by Marriott has maintained Gold Hotel Status for all but one year. In addition, its associates are involved yearround in activities that exemplify Marriott's spirit to serve. These include various fundraising events to benefit the University of Virginia Children's Hospital and the United Way.

Residence Inn by Marriott provides residential-style lodging for extended-stay business travelers. With more than fifty percent more space than the average hotel accommodation, guests have plenty of room to work and relax in oversized studio suites and one- and two-bedroom suites.

Residence Inn by Marriott hotels is architecturally and environmentally designed to resemble an upscale residential complex and is designed particularly for extended-stay travelers.

Features include complimentary hot breakfast, an evening hospitality hour, swimming pool, sport court, personalized grocery shopping, daily housekeeping, fully equipped kitchens, and work space with free high-speed Internet access and voice mail.

The Residence Inn by Marriott is operated by Marriott International, Inc., a leading worldwide hospitality company. The firm's heritage may be traced to a Washington, D.C., root beer stand opened in 1927 by J. Willard and Alice Marriott.

Today, Marriott International operates nearly 2,800 lodging properties across the United States and in 69 other countries and territories.

Residence Inn was the first hotel company to coin the term "extended stay" in 1975. In 1987, Marriott purchased the 96-property Residence Inn Corporation and today there are more than 425 Residence Inn by Marriott hotels in the United States, Canada and Mexico.

The Charlottesville location of Residence Inn by Marriott at 1111 Millmont Street has become one of the most popular destinations for extended stay visitors to the area.

MARTHA JEFFERSON HOUSE

Martha Jefferson House, a unique retirement community, has provided gracious living for seniors and retirees since 1957. Residents of Martha Jefferson House maintain an independent lifestyle, yet have personal services and support readily available when needed.

Martha Jefferson House is built around a beautiful Georgian-Style home constructed in 1921. The spacious grounds and gardens provide a warm, home-like atmosphere. In addition to tastefully appointed suites, the home includes assisted living accommodations and The Infirmary, a highly regarded nursing facility. A planned expansion will include accommodations adjoining the original house.

The concept for Martha Jefferson House was conceived by Charlottesville philanthropists Hunter Perry and his sister, Lillian Perry Edwards, who bequeathed the mansion, along with a substantial endowment, to provide gracious living for those who desire to live independently, but not alone.

The home was originally donated to Martha Jefferson Hospital and was operated by the hospital until June 2000. At that time the home separated from the hospital and became an independently governed organization.

Located on a private cul-de-sac at 1600 Gordon Avenue, in the heart of the University of Virginia neighborhood, Martha Jefferson House is surrounded by stately trees and aged English boxwoods that provide an ambiance of perennial peace. It is situated in an area of historical significance dating from the days of Thomas Jefferson.

Residents of Martha Jefferson House live together much as a family, each enjoying his or her own hobbies, work, and activities, but sharing each other's company. Residents have the time and space to enjoy life independently, with as much or as little support as they desire.

Martha Jefferson House is a private, nonprofit endeavor and, as such, does not accept Medicare or Medicaid reimbursements. Staffing is greater per resident than most retirement facilities, offering the very best in care to residents and a high level of maintenance for the home and grounds. Those who have lived at Martha Jefferson House over the years would agree that this House is truly a home.

When you have an unusual name it's nice to have a good story to go with it.

When A. Scott Ward was born at home in downtown Scottsville in 1936, his father and the doctor celebrated the great occasion with some of "the local recipe." When the time came to fill out the certificate of live birth, both men were feeling pretty good. Somehow, Scott's name got mixed up in the name column and the first name was spelled incorrectly. Thus he was officially named Alexandria Scottsville Ward.

Scott was unaware of the error until he joined the Air Force in 1953. When he asked his Mom about the name she replied, "Oh, son, we always meant to change that." It never did get changed. He now goes by the name of A. Scott Ward, but you don't want to call him Alexandria.

Scott is the joint owner of A. Scott Ward Realty, Inc., a family business that includes his business partner and wife, Frankie; their daughter, Jeannette Kerlin, who serves as office manager; and her husband, Bo Kerlin, who is managing broker of the Scottsville sales office. There also is Frankie's sister, Dolores Rogers, an agent; and a great niece, Angela Tooley, who is the company receptionist. Once an agent affiliates with the firm they become part of the family as well. The office motto is "We Treat People Like Family."

"We think the Scottsville area represents the best buy in real estate," Scott says. "It's a different way of life here. Very laid back, no

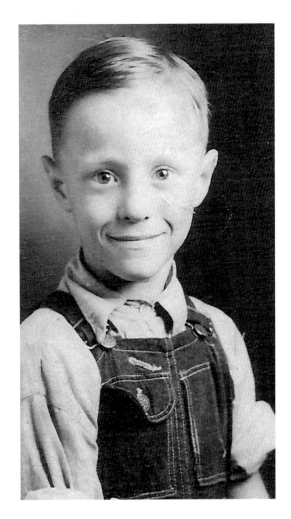

traffic lights and everyone knows your name. In Albemarle County, this is the place to live."

Although Scott is a specialist in property around Scottsville, the firm is also active in Charlottesville, Fluvanna, Cumberland, Louisa, Greene, and other counties. The firm opened a branch office in Dillwyn, Buckingham County in January 2003 with Chris Vance as managing broker.

Scott has served on the Scottsville Chamber of Commerce as vice president, is a past-president of the Scottsville Lions Club, member of the Victory Theater restoration committee and has served on many committees of the Scottsville United Methodist Church where he currently serves as administrative chairperson.

The real estate business and the community of Scottsville have served Scott Ward well. "I like helping people buy and sell homes," he says. "And I like the flexibility my real estate career has given me."

For information about real estate in the Scottsville area, please call A. Scott Ward at 434-286-2022 or visit www.scottward.com.

❖

A. Scott Ward.

HERITAGE
MEMORIALS,
INC.

❖

Heritage Memorials, Inc.'s
Charlottesville showroom at 1640
East Rio Road.

Heritage Memorials opened its Charlottesville location in 1984 at 1640 East Rio Road but the business actually dates back to 1874 and the establishment of Samuel Loewner Monuments in Harrisonburg, Virginia.

Several generations of the Loewner family operated the business until 1962 when it was sold and renamed James H. Bryan Memorials. In 1973, Jeanne H. Rinker, who was the twenty-three year-old secretary for Bryan Memorials, purchased the business and later changed the name to Heritage Memorials, Inc. During the next thirty years the business grew to annual sales of $1.5 million.

Heritage Memorials provides beautiful, timeless monuments for more than seven hundred cemeteries in eighteen counties. The Charlottesville location serves Albemarle, Greene, Madison, Orange, Louisa, Nelson,

Fluvanna, and Buckingham Counties. Locations in Harrisonburg, Staunton and Waynesboro serve other counties in the Shenandoah Valley and in West Virginia. Heritage Memorials is equipped with the newest equipment and computers to assist skilled artists and engravers in creating a beautiful and lasting memorial.

An enormous amount of work goes into the making of a memorial and the engraving process at Heritage Memorials has many steps. A skilled craftsman performs each step to produce a memorial that is a work of art of which the family will be proud.

Heritage Memorials is the authorized regional distributor for Rock of Ages monuments, whose quality and workmanship are second to none. Rock of Ages Corporation was founded in 1885 and furnishes a warranty that remains in effect forever. In addition, Heritage Memorials carries many colors of granite from quarries all over the world.

The two key ingredients in selection of a monument are quality granite and superior workmanship. The trained sales staff at Heritage Memorials will help you design a creative personalized memorial for your loved one. Their dedication to excellence assures you your choice will be a comfort to all.

Memorial selection for a loved one can be difficult, but Heritage Memorials offers their years of experience and the finest granites to help preserve a lifetime of memories.

Heritage Memorials of Charlottesville is located at the intersection of Route 29 North and Rio Road at 1640 East Rio Road in Charlottesville, Virginia. Heritage Memorials can be found on the Internet at www.heritage-memorials.com.

Innisfree was established in 1971 when a group of concerned parents in northern Virginia gathered to plan for the future of their sons and daughters, young adults with mental disabilities who were facing an uncertain future.

At that time there were few satisfactory residential, recreational or vocational options for people with mental disability. The founders—Mark and Barbara Fried, Heinz and Alice Kramp, Hank and Gerald Luria, Mr. and Mrs. Hermon Miller, and Tom and Sherry Nicholson—began working with Heinz Kramp, who became Innisfree's first director.

The group preferred a rural setting close to a major medical facility and settled on the Charlottesville area, where they found Walnut Level Farm in Brown's Cove. That same year, Heinz and his family moved into the old farm house with two coworkers, as Innisfree residents are known. Shortly thereafter the residents began baking bread, gardening and weaving.

Innisfree's first house and bakery were located in Walnut Level, one of the original Brown family plantation houses. The original part of the home was built in the late 1700s and there is an historic family graveyard behind the house. Innisfree is located on 550 acres at the foot of the Shenandoah National Park, one of the most beautiful settings in Albemarle County.

Innisfree now consists of nine residential buildings, a community center, office building and a variety of workshops. Other coworkers live and work in two houses in a downtown neighborhood.

The facility consists of 39 coworkers, 15 full-time residential volunteers and, 10 staff members.

In addition to baking and weaving, coworkers are involved in such activities as Meals on Wheels, serving as a teacher's helper at Beth Israel Preschool, volunteering at Martha Jefferson Hospital, working as an activity assistant at the Christopher Center at Our Lady of Peace, and the Special Olympics. The Innisfree community has raised funds for Church World Service Disaster Relief, the Salvation Army Christmas Drive, Shelter for Help in Emergency, Interfaith Action for Homeless Children, Presbyterian Family and Home Services and the Crozet Headstart program.

Innisfree is dedicated to providing a life-sharing home and work environment in an atmosphere of beauty, warmth and respectfulness. All community members are valued and all are encouraged to explore a meaningful and challenging life.

Above: Smiles in the weavery.

Below: "Where peace comes dropping slow."

JOHN LINKOUS VOLKSWAGEN, INC.

Few businesses in the Albemarle County area are better known or more highly respected than John Linkous Volkswagen.

When John Linkous established the business in 1974, his automotive experience included work with a Volkswagen dealer during the 1960s, when the popular autos were first introduced into this country. The business opened at 918 Preston Avenue on August 1, 1974. The dealership moved to its present location at 1313 Richmond Road on Pantops Mountain in 1979.

The dealership added Mazda vehicles to its line in 1976.

John Linkous Volkswagen was a family-run business for many years, with daughter Kathy Linkous Simmons joining the dealership in 1984 and son Doug Linkous coming into the business in 1989. It remained a family operated business for three years after the death of John Linkous in 2000.

The dealership was sold in 2003 to Flow Companies of Winston-Salem, North Carolina.

Throughout his long career, John Linkous took great pride in providing customers with exceptional service. This attitude helped the dealership attract, and keep, many long-time customers.

One of the dealership's longtime customers shared this story with John's wife, Shirley,

following his death. It seems the customer had purchased a used vehicle and had been informed that the car was in tip-top shape. However, the customer soon discovered that a door wasn't working right and the engine was running rough. He returned the car to the service manager, who looked it over and informed him that the car needed several hundred dollars worth of work.

"That didn't seem right," the customer wrote, "so I knocked on John's door and handed him both the sales receipt and the service report. I was just beginning to explain my side of the story when he jumped up and marched to the service desk. 'Fix this man's car,' he said in a firm tone. 'Fix everything, and don't charge him anything.'"

"The whole operation—problem, analysis, solution—took John only about thirty seconds, but it kept me coming back for almost thirty years," the customer continued.

John Linkous established this reputation for superior customer service when he first opened his doors in 1974 and that heritage still guides the current owners of John Linkous VW/Mazda.

❖

Above: President John D. Linkous.

Below: John Linkous VW/Mazda dealership is located at 1313 Richmond Road in Charlottesville, Virginia.

Since it was founded in downtown Charlottesville in 1913, the Charlottesville Regional Chamber of Commerce has been dedicated to representing private enterprise, promoting business and enhancing the quality of life in the greater Charlottesville communities.

As the region's premier business and civic organization, the Chamber is committed to helping members improve their businesses. To this end, the Chamber offers its twelve hundred members a variety of networking opportunities, referrals and up-to-date business data.

The Chamber's networking events attract more than four thousand people each year. At the same time, more than 350 members enhance their business skills through a variety of workshops, seminars and forums.

One of the Chamber's most important functions is serving as an advocate for business interests in the Charlottesville region. The Chamber's Board of Directors, committee members and staff are actively engaged in public policy matters, both locally and at the state level.

Because building the community helps sustain and strengthen the region's overall economic vitality, the Chamber and its members have led successful community building activities for more than nine decades.

Chamber leadership has helped organize, lead and sustain many key community organizations, including United Way, Charlottesville Albemarle Convention & Visitors Bureau, Charlottesville Area School Business Alliance, Leadership Charlottesville, Thomas Jefferson Partnership for Economic Development, Free Enterprise Forum, Business Education Round Table, North Charlottesville Business Council and other business and civic councils and round tables.

Although a skilled and experienced staff operates the Chamber, the real power of Chamber enterprises lies in its members. Chamber business volunteers are recognized as key business and civic leaders in building and sustaining the economic vitality and quality of life in the Charlottesville region.

Chamber members are involved at every level in assessing risks and implementing new business enterprises in the community. The Chamber will continue to play a pivotal role as the area's economy continues to evolve toward a market led by education, highly skilled technology-based jobs, retail, agribusiness and tourism.

The Charlottesville Regional Chamber of Commerce is key to building a business and building a community—two excellent reasons for any enterprise to be a Chamber member.

CHARLOTTESVILLE REGIONAL CHAMBER OF COMMERCE

BANK OF AMERICA

The Peoples Bank of Charlottesville was organized as a state bank in 1875, the first bank formed in Charlottesville following the closing of area banks after the end of the War Between the States.

It was originally financed in 1875 by the sale of common stock to approximately twenty original stockholders, with a capital of $20,000. The president was A. R. Blakey and directors were R. G. Crank, H. Clay Marchant, C. H. Harman, Simon Leterman, L. T. Hanckel, A. J. Farish, Jas T. Durrette, Edward Coles, Benjamin R. Pace, J. Augustus Michie, Jesse W. Jones and Charles Goodyear.

For two years, the bank occupied the building on the corner of Market and Fourth Streets. The second location in 1895 was on the corner of Main and Fourth, now Timberlake's Drug Store.

Judge John M. White became president in January 1895 and served until his death in 1913. George R. B. Michie, who served until shortly before his death in 1938, succeeded him.

Through mergers, the Peoples National Bank of Charlottesville became Peoples National Bank of Central Virginia in 1962. In 1963 through the merger and consolidation with National Bank of Commerce of Norfolk, Virginia, the Virginia National Bank was formed. William S. Hildreth succeeded George Michie.

Hildreth later became chairman of the board and W. Wright Harrison served as president from 1957 until 1963.

A merger of Virginia National Bank and First & Merchant of Richmond on December 31, 1983, created the Sovran Bank. C&S/Sovran combined later with the North Carolina Bank Corporation to form NationsBank on December 31, 1991.

Throughout its history, the bank has helped preserve local heritage and open opportunities for individuals, the community and institutions such as the University of Virginia. It underwrote the bond issue to restore the University's Rotunda after the fire of 1895. It funded the publication of *Early Charlottesville: Recollections of James Alexander 1825-1874*, and led in the establishment of the University of Virginia Graduate School of Business and in raising funds for University Hall. NationsBank was a significant contributor to the restoration of the McIntire Building. The bank began financing automobiles for purchasers as early as 1915.

On October 1, 1998, NationsBank merged with BankAmerica Corporation of San Francisco to create the new coast-to-coast Bank of America, a highly diversified and dominant franchise that is the nation's largest bank.

For more information and locations of Bank of America, please visit www.bankofamerica.com.

Carmello's is the sort of Italian restaurant you've always longed for. It's a family restaurant where the owner greets you at the door and his wife and children are actually in the kitchen preparing authentic dishes that could never be duplicated at a chain restaurant.

Bill Hedges moved his restaurant to Charlottesville twelve years ago after establishing a reputation for fine dining in northern Virginia. The spacious restaurant at 400 Emmett Street can seat eighty-five people in rustic, comfortable, but still elegant surroundings.

Carmello's offers northern Italian cuisine with hints of central and southern Italian influence. Specialties include fresh fish, veal, chicken and rack of lamb. An extensive wine list is available, complete with labels and detailed descriptions.

Restaurant reviewers from Washington to Charlottesville have praised Carmello's. One reviewer wrote, "Carmello's has discovered the secret that makes a restaurant successful—each time you leave you think the food and service couldn't get any better, but each time you return you discover that it has."

Hedges, whose heritage is "half-Italian and half-Greek" grew up in Montreal, Canada and has been in the restaurant business since 1959. "I started in Montreal and worked my way through New Jersey, New York, and Washington, D.C., operating several restaurants along the way," he explains.

Hedges is a chef and both he and his wife, Stella, work in the kitchen, overseeing the preparation of each dish. Their son, George, is also an accomplished chef and has worked in the family business since childhood. Hedges expects that his son will take over the restaurant some day and keep the traditions alive. A daughter, Irene, also works at the restaurant part-time.

"George started at a young age and is very good in the kitchen," says Hedges. "One day a customer was raving about how delicious the food was and insisted on meeting the chef. She was flabbergasted to discover he was only fourteen years old."

Many discriminating diners consider Carmello's the finest restaurant in Charlottesville and over the years the restaurant has developed a loyal clientele.

"When we established Carmello's, we wanted to offer something entirely different from the chain restaurants," Hedges explains. "We wanted a restaurant where you are greeted by name and where the food is fresh and well prepared and the service is always prompt and friendly."

The dining room at Carmello's can seat eighty-five.

BLUE RIDGE HOME BUILDERS ASSOCIATION

The Blue Ridge Home Builders Association (BRHBA) is dedicated to preserving and promoting the American dream of home ownership.

The Association was organized in 1964 to unite builder/developers with allied trade industries, businesses and professions in the building industry. BRHBA represents members in Charlottesville and the Albemarle, Fluvanna, Greene, Madison and Nelson Counties

BRHBA maintains an active Governmental Affairs Committee that monitors local, stateand national regulations affecting the homebuilding industry. These efforts are closely coordinated with the statewide Home Builders Association of Virginia(HBAV), which is listed as one of the top\ten most effective lobbying groups n the state.

In addition, BRHBA participates in the Free Enterprise Forum, a joint coalition of the Regional Chamber of Commerce and the Charlottesville Area Association of Realtors to monitor legislation that affects our communities.

Regular BRHBA membership meetings provide members an opportunity for networking and continuing education.

Thousands of area residents attend BRHBA's annual Parade of Homes, a showcase of the latest styles and trends in home building that helps promote new home sales.

The Home Show sponsored by BRHBA attracts more than three thousand visitors each March and is the largest, longest running exhibition in Charlottesville.

BRHBA's annual Membership Directory is a "who's who" of the local building industry, listing all member firms with contact names, addresses, phone and fax numbers and e-mail and website addresses.

Membership in BRHBA is open to homebuilders, remodelers and developers. Associate memberships are offered for businesses allied with the homebuilding industry, such as finance and insurance firms, law firms, utilities and others.

BRHBA membership includes membership in the Home Builders Association of Virginia (HBAV) and the National Association of Home Builders (NAHB). All three organizations offer resources for legal, marketing, technological and product assistance, as well as training and educational opportunities. In addition, the association offers several insurance programs for its members, including builder's risk/liability, workman's compensation and health, life and disability.

The Blue Ridge Home Builders Association is located at 233 Commonwealth Drive, Suite 100, Charlottesville, Virginia 22901. The association's website is www.brhb.org.

Gold's Gym has been the authority on fitness since 1965. Today, Gold's Gym is the largest co-ed gym chain in the world with over 600 facilities in 43 states and 25 countries.

Celebrity endorsers of Gold's Gym include Arnold Schwarzenegger, who moved to the United States to work out at the original Gold's Gym in Venice, California. Also, celebrities as diverse as Mel Gibson and Bruce Springsteen, Nadia Comaneci, Michael Jordan, and hundreds of others rely on Gold's Gym to meet their fitness needs.

Since it opened in 1992, Gold's Gym Charlottesville has been the choice for thousands of Charlottesville and Albemarle County residents who have relied on the facilities and expertise of Gold's Gym for the results they want.

Gold's Gym offers one-on-one orientations with personal trainers, fitness assessment follow-ups, group fitness classes for all levels and interests, as well as nutrition consultants. Clients find that Gold's Gym provides the results they want in meeting their fitness goals.

An extensive selection of exercise equipment, including Cybex, Hammer Strength, Precor, Quentin, Nautilus, Life Fitness and Body Masters, provide both cardiovascular and strength workouts.

Gold's Gym will soon move to a much larger thirty-five-thousand-square-foot-facility that will include three separate group fitness studios, a Lady Gold's for women only, in-house chiropractic and sports medicine, a Planet Smoothie wireless Internet café, and the finest Kidz Club in town, replete with movie theatre, half-court basketball hoops, tube crawl, wall climb, homework stations, and the best in Kidz exercise.

Gold's Gym continues to change lives by helping people achieve their individual potential. Members of Gold's Gym lose forty-four thousand pounds of fat a day, enough to make a difference in the health of the world.

Above: Gold's Gym is located at 153 Zan Road in Charlottesville, Virginia.

Below: (From left to right) Rebecca Dail, Eddie Dail, Kali Gustafson, and Kevin Gustafson.

SPONSORS

A. Scott Ward 111

ACAC Fitness and Wellness Centers 80

Albemarle Charlottesville Historical Society 98

Albemarle County 90

Allied Concrete Company 94

Bank of America 116

Blue Ridge Home Builders Association 118

Boar's Head Inn 99

Carlisle Motion Control Industries, Inc. 100

Carmello's 117

City of Charlottesville 91

Charlottesville Regional Chamber of Commerce 115

Chase Investment Counsel Corporation 92

Core Knowledge Foundation 76

Gold's Gym 119

Hampton Inn & Suites at the University 82

Hantzmon Wiebel, L.L.P. 105

Heritage Memorials, Inc. 112

Hospice of the Piedmont 96

Innisfree, Inc. 113

John Linkous Volkswagen, Inc. 114

Martha Jefferson House 110

McGuireWoods L.L.P. 108

McLean Faulconer, Inc. 106

Mincer's University of Virginia Imprinted Sportswear 103

NAEVA Geophysics, Inc. 86

Our Lady of Peace 104

Residence Inn by Marriott 71, 109

Richard A. Oliva & Sons, Inc. 88

Richmond & Fishburne, L.L.P. 101

Rivanna Farm 84

Stevens & Company 102

Thomas Jefferson Foundation 79

W. A. Lynch Roofing Company, Inc. 107

W. E. Brown, Inc. 72